Grow and Cook

By
Brian Tucker

Published by The Good Life Press Ltd. 2008

Copyright © Brian Tucker

ISBN 978 1 90487 136 1
A catalogue record for this book is available from the British Library.

Published by
The Good Life Press Ltd.
PO Box 536
Preston
PR2 9ZY

www.thegoodlifepress.co.uk

Set by The Good Life Press Ltd.
Printed and bound in Great Britain by Creative Print & Design.

Grow and Cook

Simple Recipes from Seed to Plate

By
Brian Tucker

Contents

Herbs

Appendicies

Introduction

Who could possibly be interested in a book that isn't either a gardening encyclopaedia or a cook's recipe book, but a combination of them both?

Well, as both a professional chef and a professional gardener people have often asked me questions such as, "How do I cook the unusual or different vegetables that my husband has decided to grow?" or alternatively, "My wife enjoys cooking different and usual dishes, so what can I grow to encourage her?" I have even been asked, "What can I grow and what should I do with it when I have grown it?"

It would appear then that a great many people are interested in both gardening and cookery, so I decided to sit down and try to compile this book.

The growing methods and the recipes that I have used throughout 'Grow and Cook' are just the basic and most usual ways of producing reasonable quality crops and interesting cuisine. I was born and brought up in the country, in Devonshire, and have spent many, many happy years working the soil and many of my recipes reflect a simple way of life.

I do not expect it to win any awards. The greatest satisfaction is that their simplicity should make even the most reluctant gardener-come-cook want to have a go.

Always remember though, that the art of both growing and cooking are achieved largely by experimentation. I have taken for granted that the grower is conversant with the usual principles of soil preparation, terminology etc. so I have not dealt at length with this and nor have I dwelt on basic cookery theories. So much is common sense.

I would like to extend my grateful thanks to any of my friends and associates who have given me advice and/or help in producing this work with a very, very big thank you to my wife, Beryl, who put up with me and encouraged me continuously over the years. But alas she has now passed away.

So good growing and even better eating!

Brian Tucker, Barnstaple, 2008

Editors note: *When Brian's manuscript arrived, all neatly typed up with his notes in the margins we decided to keep the imperial measurements in, mainly because, oddly, gardening seems to have avoided the conversion; a 3" pot, for instance, is still referred to as a 3" pot, not an 8cm pot and many instructions on the backs of seed packets remain in inches.*

For those more used to the metric measurements Brian says good luck to you and you can find an easy conversion chart at the end of the book.

Artichokes | Globe

"It has the virtue of . . . provoking Venus for both men and women; for women making them more desirable, and helping the men who are in these matters rather tardy." From the 'Book of Nature,' by Dr. Bartolomeo Boldo in 1576.

Also called the 'French artichoke' or the 'green artichoke,' it derives its common name from the northern Italian words *articiocco* and *articoclos*. This latter term is supposed to come from the word *cocali,* meaning a pine cone.

The artichoke is a perennial in the thistle group of the sunflower family and is believed to be a native of the Mediterranean and the Canary Islands. In full growth the plant spreads to cover an area about 6ft in diameter and reaches a height of 3 to 4ft. The 'vegetable' that we eat is actually the plant's flower bud. If allowed to flower the blossoms measure up to seven inches in diameter and are a beautiful violet-blue colour.

Planting

Globe artichokes can be grown from seed sown outside in April, but this is not really to be recommended as it will take several years to produce a useable crop. A far better method is to plant offsets which are really suckers from a parent plant. These offsets are best planted in early April on a well-manured site, allowing a minimum of 30" around each plant. Mulch well in May and remove all the flower heads in this first season. Remove all dead and dying leaves in autumn and protect againt frost. The following spring feed with a general fertiliser at the rate of 2 to 3oz to the square yard.

Harvesting

Start cropping the flower heads in July and before they start turning brown at the edges. The King Crown, or large central head, should always be the first one harvested.

Globe artichokes crop best in their second and third years, so it is best to replace them every three years. To achieve annual crops it is preferable to have three beds in varying ages in operation at any one time. Allow one head per portion. Choose heavy compact heads that yield slightly to the touch. A good sample has green, tightly closed leaf scales.

Preparing

Prepare immediately before cooking. Remove the top inch of the head using a sharp knife. Trim back the stalk to within an inch of the bottom and remove any loose leaves. Clip off the tips of all other leaves. The heads are now ready for cooking.

Cooking

Drop the heads into salted, boiling water. Season each

head further by adding a small garlic clove, a slice of lemon and a tablespoon of vegetable oil. Cover and boil until the stem can be easily pierced with a fork. Remove from the water and drain well. Remove the stub of the stalk.

To serve as a hot vegetable
Place upright on a plate and serve with hot melted butter, mayonnaise or hollandaise sauce.

To serve as a salad
Drain and chill the cooked artichokes. Place them upright on a plate. Serve with mayonnaise blended with lemon juice and prepared English mustard. This makes an excellent starter, either hot or cold.

A Tip on Eating Globe Artichokes
Pull off each leaf individually and dip the light coloured end into the sauce. Only eat the tender part of the leaf by drawing through the teeth. Discard the tip. When all the leaves have been eaten in this way, remove the centre choke from the heart which is then cut up, dipped in the sauce and eaten.

Italian Style
Prepare as before! Stand in 1½″ of salted, boiling water, add the cut off stems, cover and cook for about 30 minutes. Drain, peel and chop the stems. Sauté two chopped onions and 2 garlic cloves in one tablespoon of oil until yellow. Add the stems and 2 teaspoons of chopped parsley, 4oz of chopped celery, 8 chopped anchovies, 4 teaspoons of grated parmesan cheese, 3oz of soft bread crumbs and 3

teaspoons of capers. Add salt and pepper to taste.

Spread the leaves of the cooked artichoke and remove the choke. Fill the cavity left with the above mixture. Any spaces at the base of any large leaves can also be stuffed.

Place in a baking tin, cover the bottom of the tin with a little water and pour a little oil over each head. Cover and bake in a moderate oven (350°F/Gas mark 4) until very tender. The amounts given would be sufficient for 4 large or 8 small artichokes or 4 servings.

Artichoke hearts can also be coated in breadcrumbs and deep fried as a starter.

Preserving

You should really eat the artichoke as soon as possible because the flavour does subdue once it has been cut off the stalk. You can keep them in the fridge for up to 5 days, unwashed, in a bag.

Artichokes can be frozen after cooking. Do not freeze them raw as they turn brown on thawing and the taste isn't very pleasent.

Artichoke | Jerusalem

The Jerusalem artichoke has no connection with the

city of its name and nor is it an artichoke. It is actually a relation of the sunflower. This plant, which grows to about 5ft high, is grown for its tubers which look like gnarled white potatoes, but they are smaller and more watery, with a taste similar to cooked chestnuts.

Planting

To grow them is fairly easy. Plant the tubers in rows 30 inches apart with the tubers 15" apart and about 4" deep. Hoe occasionally, drawing the soil towards the plants. Pinch out any flower buds that appear to encourage tuber production.

Harvesting

Harvesting can commence in the autumn and through the winter. If possible it is best to lift the tubers as required. One advantage of this crop is that the tops make a very effective screen during the summer months.

Preparing

Wash and then peel them. Peeling is not easy due to the knobbly bits. Once peeled they can be left whole, halved, sliced or grated.

Cooking

Cook until tender in boiling salted water for about 15 to

20 minutes. Do NOT overcook this vegetable. Drain, add 2oz of butter, 2 tablespoons of lemon juice, 2 tablespoons of chopped parsley, a dash of cayenne pepper and cook for a further 3 minutes. Serve as any usual vegetable.

Jerusalem artichokes are also very nice par-boiled and then roasted for the last 20 minutes or so with the joint and meat juices.

Jerusalem Artichoke Soup

Peel as best you, can then grate 1lb of artichokes. Put in a colander and press to squeeze out as much of the water as possible. Lightly fry an onion with some garlic, pepper and salt in oil or butter in a pan.

Add the grated artichokes, allowing the mixture to sweat for 5 minutes.

Add a pint of chicken stock and cook on a low heat until soft enough to blend.

Put into a blender or hand blend until smooth.

Add cream and serve with hot bread and butter.

Asparagus

The word asparagus comes from the Greek *inasparagos*, meaning to shoot, or sprout. Asparagus spears are, in fact, edible shoots that develop on rhizomes when the soil temperature is warm and the water supply is favourable. The spears, if not harvested, develop into ferns some 4 to 6ft tall. It is a hardy perennial vegetable native to the seacoasts of Europe and eastern Asia, where it has been cultivated for over 2,000 years. It was a vegetable well-known and valued by both the Greeks and the Romans.

Growing

Asparagus is another very long term crop, so good preparation of the plot is essential. Although asparagus can be grown from seed, it is more usual to plant 1 or 2 year old seedling crowns. These are normally planted in 4ft wide beds with 3 rows to a bed, the crowns being 15" apart in the rows.

Dig out a trench 8 to 10" deep and 12" wide. Form a small ridge along the bottom of this trench. Place the crowns on this ridge with the string like roots spread out evenly on each side of the ridge. Cover with about 3 to 4" of soil.

While hoeing during the growing season, gradually fill in the trench.

Each autumn and spring draw up the earth over the rows in the same manner as used for potatoes.

Feed the bed each spring with a general fertiliser and mulch well in the autumn with well-rotted manure or compost.

Cut off all top growth in November.

Harvesting

Do not attempt to harvest any spears of asparagus the first year, but a year after planting it is possible to cut 1 central shoot from each crown. The next year you can harvest all of the shoots that are available over a four week period which will extend to six weeks in ensuing years.

Never harvest any spears after the middle of June.

To gather the crop, cut the spears 2 to 3″ below the surface of the bed when the shoots are about 5″ high, thus giving a total spear length of approximately 7½″.

Preparing

The stalk should be green and tender for most of its length, with close, compact tips. Allow 2lbs for 4 servings.

Trim off the tough ends and remove any large scales along the stalk that might hold some grit. Wash thoroughly to remove all grit and then tie into bunches.

Cooking

Stand the bundles upright in a deep saucepan. Add boiling salted water until about 1″ deep. Cover tightly and boil until just tender (approximately 10 to 15 minutes). If the stalks are a bit coarse they can be gently peeled and cooked horizontally. Peeled spears will be slightly more tender.

Asparagus can also be cut into 1″ lengths before boiling or can be steamed in a steamer where it should only need cooking for about half the above time.

Serving Ideas
Remove from the water carefully to avoid breaking the spears. Drain well and serve at once with either melted butter or hollandaise sauce.

Alternatively, the cooked spears can be dipped into beaten egg and fine bread crumbs before deep frying for approximately 3 minutes until lightly browned.

The cooked asparagus can also be sprinkled with Parmesan cheese and melted butter before lightly grilling to a delicate brown. Asparagus can also be served as a creamed vegetable. To do this chop the cooked asparagus spears into 1 inch pieces. Dice some hard boiled egg and fold it with the asparagus pieces into a rich white sauce. Reheat and serve at once on slices of toast.

Preserving

Asparagus needs moisture and therefore I don't recommend that you store them for long. You can put the stalks, standing up straight like a bunch of flowers in a vase, in a jar of water. Cover the tips with a plastic bag and leave in the coldest part of the refrigerator for about 2 days.

If you are short of space I wouldn't really advise you to plant asparagus as it does not make good use of your land as yields are limited and preserving is minimal.

Aubergines | Eggplants

Southeast Asia has always been considered as the possible place of the eggplant's origin because of the many varieties found there. The egg plant arrived on the European scene when the Moors invaded Spain during the 8th Century. The Italians encountered the fruit through trading with the Arabs in about the 13th Century. What the Europeans saw with the first arrivals of eggplant were egg-shaped fruits that were either purple, white, or yellow.

Planting

The aubergine, or eggplant, can be grown easily, although the plants do need the protection of a greenhouse in the early stages. The seeds are sown 2 to 3 to a 3″ pot in a heated greenhouse in early April.

When the seedlings emerge they should be thinned to the strongest one in each pot. Care given to feeding and watering at this time will pay dividends at a later date as it will build up strong plants capable of producing their full cropping potential.

In early June when the plants are about 8 to 10″ high, they should be transplanted 3ft apart all round into their cropping site which should have been well- prepared and manured.

As soon as the plants have settled in, pinch out the growing tip to encourage the plant to produce sideshoots and to branch out into a bush shape. Water well and feed weekly.

Harvesting

Aubergines will start cropping in July/August and should yield until mid October or even later if it is a mild season. Harvest regularly as soon as the fruits are ready.

Aubergines should be a clear, dark purple glossy colour that covers the entire surface. Beware of picking aubergines that are too big as they are inclined to be tough. An average size would be about 1½lbs in weight and should serve 4.

Preparing

Very little preparation is required with aubergines as, unless the skin is exceptionally tough, there is no need to peel the vegetable. Just give them a good wash but do not soak in salt water before cooking.

Cooking

Aubergines can be grilled, sautéed, baked, stuffed or casseroled so it is quite a versatile vegetable.

To Grill
Slice them in ½″ slices, brush with melted butter or bacon

fat, place them under the grill and cook until brown on both sides. Serve hot with grilled meat.

Sautéed Aubergine

Slice the aubergine into ½" slices. Dip in fine breadcrumbs, then beaten egg and again in fine bread crumbs. Season, fry slowly in very little oil until brown and transparent looking. Turn and brown on the side. Serve hot. Aubergines can also be deep-fried in this way.

Stuffed Aubergines

Cut two small aubergines in half, lengthways and simmer in salted water for about 10 minutes until almost tender.

Sauté 1oz of chopped green pepper, 1oz of chopped onion and 1oz of diced celery until golden brown. Combine with a large can of condensed tomato soup, 8oz of cooked rice, a dash of thyme and salt and pepper to taste.

Scoop out the centre of the aubergines leaving a half inch of pulp around the sides.
Sprinkle a few crushed cream cracker crumbs over the bottom of each shell, fill with the rice mixture and cover with more crumbs.

Dot with butter and bake in a moderate oven (375°F/Gas Mark 4) for 30 minutes. Serve at once.

Baked Aubergines

Marinate the sliced aubergine in French dressing for about 15 minutes. Drain and spread with softened butter. Bake in a hot oven (400°F/Gas mark 6) for approximately 15 minutes until tender turning once. Sprinkle with lemon juice and serve immediately.

Italian Aubergine Casserole

Wash the aubergine thoroughly, then slice it 4 inches thick. Dip the slices into a batter made by blending a well beaten egg, 3fl oz of milk and 1½ teaspoons of salt. Brown in a frying pan with 2oz of butter or dripping.

Place a layer of the browned aubergine slices in an oven proof casserole dish, placing thin slices of mozzarella cheese and thin slices of tomato on top of the aubergine. Sprinkle with oregano, using about half a teaspoon on each layer. Season with salt and pepper.

Repeat these layers until all the aubergine is used, finishing with a cheese layer. Pour 1 tablespoon of olive oil over the top.

Cover and bake in a moderate oven (350°F/Gas Mark 4) for about 30 minutes, removing the cover for the last ten minutes of cooking.

A garlic flavour can be added to this dish by putting crushed garlic cloves in the butter or dripping. Serve at once. One good sized aubergine should yield six average portions.

Vegetable Hotpot

Cut 3 large onions into chunks, cut a small green pepper

into very small pieces and a good sized aubergine into 1 inch cubes. Skin and roughly chop the tomatoes and crush the garlic. Heat the oil in a large, heavy based saucepan. Put in the onion and allow it to fry for 2 minutes. Add the pepper and the aubergine and mix well. Add garlic, 1 teaspoon of sugar, salt, a bay leaf and black pepper and stir well. Cover the saucepan tightly and simmer gently for about an hour. Serve with rice, pasta or large chunks of crusty French bread.

Preserving

You are best off making the aubergine into a chutney and storing it this way as the flesh, whether uncooked or cooked, does not freeze well.

Beans | Broad

The broad bean, or fava bean, has a history and is often associated with the ancient Greeks, in particular Pythagoras who had a theory that the bean had mystical properties and was best left well alone. To ensure this he prohibited its consumption.

Broad beans are a large, furry podded bean which is held in quite high esteem by epicures.

Growing

There are two types of broad bean normally grown in the kitchen garden. They are the Longpod varieties that are sown in the autumn and the Windsor types that are spring sown. Both types require well-manured, prepared seed beds and the sowing procedures are the same, except for the actual sowing time.

Draw out flat drills 3″ deep and 6″ wide, with rows 3ft apart. Place the seeds 6″ apart and staggered along the drill and cover.

When the plants have grown and set a reasonable amount of young pods, remove the growing tip of each plant.

Taller varieties may require supporting with string, especially in exposed areas and water late crops well in dry weather.

Aquaduce is a good long pod variety, while the Sutton is a good late type.

Harvesting

Harvest the pods as they become ready. Allow 3lbs in the pod for four average servings. The pods should be well-filled, crisp, and dark green in colour. The shelled bean should be plump with a tender skin which is green to greenish white, depending on the variety.

Preparing

Wash pods well and shell the beans just before cooking.

Cooking

Broad beans take approx 20 to 25 minutes to cook. They can be used as a basic vegetable or they can be used as an ingredient in other dishes, many of which are South American in origin. The Arabic nations have a dish called *ful medames* which is made from a brown variety of broad bean.

Cook broad beans in a covered pot with about 1″ of boiling salted water. Serve by seasoning with salt and pepper and coated with melted butter or cream.

Baked and Barbequed Broad Beans

Put 1lb of shelled beans into 2 pints of water. Bring to the boil. Add ½lb of diced salt pork and simmer gently until nearly tender (about 30 minutes). Fry a large chopped onion with a crushed garlic clove in hot oil for about 5 minutes. Sprinkle with 1 tablespoon of chilli powder. Stir in a large can of condensed tomato soup, add 1 teaspoon each of Worcestershire sauce and soy souce, 2 teaspoons of mixed mustard, 2oz of brown sugar and 2fl oz of lemon juice and salt.

Bring to boiling point and pour over the beans in an oven proof casserole. Bake in a moderate oven (350°F, Gas Mark 4) for 1½hours. (Serves 6)

Broad Beans in Mushroom Sauce

Cook ½lb of broad beans and drain, keeping the liquid. Add to the beans 1lb of chopped onion, 1 teaspoon of Worcestershire sauce, 1 can of condensed mushroom soup, 12fl oz of the bean liquid and season to taste with salt and pepper. Bring to the boil and serve immediately. (Serves 4)

Preserving

You can blanche the broad beans lightly and then freeze them. Alternatively, try making them into a puree.

Beans | Green

The term green bean actually covers two different types of bean, although botanically they are the same. These are the French bean and the stick or runner bean. The runner bean is more frost susceptible and therefore cannot be planted as early as the French bean, although plants can be produced in a greenhouse for planting out in June.

Growing

Both crops require well prepared, richly manured soil. French beans are sown in late April in drills 1″ deep and 18″ apart, with the seeds sown individually at 6″ intervals.

Runner beans are sown individually in a double row with 12″ between the rows and 9″ between the seeds. The seeds should be 2″ deep. If more than one double row is required, any subsequent rows should be 6ft apart.

Runner beans need to be grown up bean poles, one to each plant, and the growing tips should be removed as soon as the top of the poles is reached. It is important to ensure that these bean poles are strong and stable as a double row of well grown runner beans has a very low wind resistance and can easily be blown over.

Both types of beans require copious amount of water, while a light spraying when the plants are in bloom assists them in setting pods.

Harvesting

Pick beans as soon as a usable size to give as long a cropping season as possible. The beans should be clean and firm but tender and free from any blemishes.

Preparing

Young tender French beans only need washing and the ends nipping off. They can also be cut into 1″ pieces. Runner beans and older French beans need to have the strings around the edges removed, before slicing diagonally into thin strips.

Cooking

Cook covered in ½″ of salted, boiling water. Allow 15 to 20 minutes cooking time. Season with salt, pepper and butter.

Alternatively, bacon or ham dripping can be used as a dressing, also crumbled crisp fried bacon gives a splendid flavour.

Raw young beans can be used in mixed green salads.

Green Beans with Almonds
Arrange the cooked, seasoned green beans in a buttered casserole dish. Add a thin white sauce and cover with slivers of almonds. Bake in a hot oven (400°F, Gas Mark 6) until the almonds are golden brown. Serve immediately.

Green Beans (French style)
Cook 1 medium sliced onion, 1 diced stick of celery and 1 small chopped carrot in 3 teaspoons of butter until tender. Add 12oz of green beans and a stock cube dissolved in 2 to 3 table spoons of hot water. Simmer until the vegetables are tender.

Preserving

Both green beans and broad beans are suitable subjects for deep freezing, making sure you can eat the produce during the winter months. This is best done by spreading the prepared beans on trays while freezing. Once frozen, the beans can be packed in 1lb packs in freezer bags.

Beans | Haricot

Haricot beans are the beans made famous as baked beans.

Growing

They are grown in exactly the same way as the green French beans.

Harvesting

Harvest when the pods ripen and go brown. The beans are then removed from the pods and air dried before storing in air tight containers.

Preparing

Dried Haricot beans require soaking for several hours or overnight before cooking.

Cooking

Check that there are no blemishes or traces of mould on any of the beans. If signs of mould are apparent, check the storage conditions as it may not have been dry before storing.

Bacon and Bean Casserole

Soak 6oz of haricot beans overnight. Drain the beans.

Cut a 1lb piece of bacon into large pieces, put it into a casserole dish and surround it with beans. Then add 2 sticks of chopped celery, 1 large sliced onion, 1 level teaspoon of sugar, 1 level teaspoon of treacle, ½ a teaspoon of dry mustard and salt and pepper to taste.

Cover with cold water and a lid and bake in a low oven (300°F, Gas Mark 2) for about 4 hours, adding water as required.

One hour before the end of the cooking time, remove the lid and lift the bacon to the top. Return to the oven and continue cooking until the bacon becomes crisp.

Barbecued (Baked) Beans

Rinse 10oz of dry haricot beans, cover with 1½ pints of cold water and soak for several hours or preferably overnight. Add 1½ teaspoons of salt and bring to the boil.

Simmer for 1½ hours or until the beans are just tender. Drain, but retain a quarter pint of liquid. Partially cook 4 rashers of fat, streaky bacon and put it to one side. Chop a medium onion, crush a clove of garlic and fry them together until transparent in the bacon fat.

Add a 10½fl oz can of condensed tomato soup, 1 teaspoon of vinegar, 1 teaspoon of French mustard, 1 teaspoon of chilli seasoning and 1 teaspoon of Worcestershire sauce together with a quarter pint of bean water.

Bring to the boil, add the cooked beans and pour into a 2 pint baking dish. Cover with the partially cooked bacon and bake in a moderate oven (350°F, Gas Mark 4) for about an hour. (Serves Six)

Bean | Sprouts

Bean sprouts are exactly that. They are the cotyledon leaf shoots of the mung bean or soybean and are much used in Chinese cookery.

Growing

The easiest method of producing a continuous supply of bean sprouts is to sow the beans on a piece of flannel or other absorbent material at weekly intervals. Keep moist and place in a warm, dim situation.

Harvesting

Once the beans have germinated and produced shoots 1″ long they are ready for use. Choose fresh, crisp, white sprouts. Discard any with brown edges to the shoots.

Preparing

Rinse gently in cold water. Remove any hard seed cases

from the bottom of the shoots. Any soft cases can be ignored.

Bean shoots can be used raw in salads or cooked by either stir-frying or simmering. It is important when cooking bean sprouts to only cook them long enough to remove the raw bean flavour, while retaining a degree of crispness.

Cooking

To cook the bean sprouts by simmering, add 1lb of fresh sprouts to 6fl oz of boiling water, cover and simmer for a few minutes. Season with salt or soy sauce.

To Stir Fry

Cook all other ingredients of the dish. Just before serving, add the sprouts and fry for about 3 minutes or until just tender, stirring the whole time.

Beetroot

There are 2 types of beetroot. One is a round or globe beetroot, while the other is a long-rooted or tapering beet. The globe beetroot is probably the best one to grow for early crops and the long-rooted one for late crops and winter storage.

Growing

The seeds of both types of beet are small and nobbly and

are actually small clusters of seeds. These seeds are grown on well dug ground in drills 12″ apart and 1″ deep. The small seed clusters should be planted 2 to 3 together with 6″ between each planting. Sow from April until July to maintain a succession of roots.

Harvesting

Lift the roots as required for immediate use.

In October all remaining roots must be lifted and the tops removed before being stored in layers of sand in a shed or sheltered place. Uncover and use as required during the winter.

Fresh prime quality beetroot should have a globular shape with a smooth, firm skin and flesh. If the leaves are still attached but look poor or withered, take no notice as this will not affect the quality of the root.

Preparing

Remove all but about 1½″ of the tops. It is preferable to twist off these tops rather than cutting them with a knife. Wash the roots well. Beetroot tops are very nutritious and very palatable when cooked in the same way as spinach.

Cooking

Cook the whole beetroot in boiling salted water, ensuring

that the roots are covered during the whole cooking period of 35 to 45 minutes, or until tender. Old, woody beet will never become tender and so must be avoided. When cooked, drain, place into cold water and rub off the skin. Serve small beetroots whole. Slice or dice the larger ones. Beetroot can be served either hot or cold.

To Serve Cold
Marinate in vinegar with a sprinkle of black pepper. Reheat using melted butter, salt, pepper and lemon juice.

Pickled Beetroot
Slice the cooked beetroot and cover it with 8fl oz of vinegar which has been boiled for 5 minutes with 4oz sugar.

Citrus Beetroot
Mix 2 tablespoons of sugar, 1 tablespoon of cornflour and 4 teaspoons of salt in a saucepan. Drain a 1lb can of grapefruit segments and stir the syrup into the cornflour mixture. Add 2fl oz of vinegar and place over a medium heat to cook, stirring constantly until the mixture boils. Allow it to boil for no more than ½ a minute. Add 1lb of whole, small or sliced beetroots. Reheat to serving temperature, add the grapefruit segments and serve. (Serves 6)

Sweet and Sour Beetroot
Mix 4oz of sugar, 2oz of flour, 2fl oz of water and 4fl oz of vinegar and cook on a medium heat until thickened (about 10 minutes). Add ½ a teaspoon of salt, 2 tablespoons of butter and 1¾ and ¼ lb of diced beetroot and cover and

cook for a further 10 minutes. (serves 4)

Hot Beetroot
Chose even sized beetroot. Remove the tops and root without breaking the skin. Wash well. Place in a large saucepan, cover with water and bring to the boil. Allow to simmer gently for 1½ hours or until the beetroot are tender. Drain, peel and keep warm. Serve with a white sauce.

Broccoli

At one time broccoli was the name used to describe the close headed winter cauliflowers as well as the various sprouting varieties such as calabrese or green, purple and white sprouting broccoli. However it is now the modern trend to restrict the name to the sprouting varieties, especially the green sprouting calabrese.

They are all members of the brassica family, which includes cabbages, brussel sprouts, savoy cabbage, mustard, turnips and wallflowers. There are many similar cultivation details which all of these crops have in common, the main one being that they all demand a rich, well firmed soil. It is best, if possible, to prepare the sites for these crops as far in advance of planting as possible.

It was George Bush Snr. who was quoted as saying that now that he was US President he no longer had to eat Brocolli!

Growing

The seeds are sown in a specially prepared seedbed. They are sown in shallow drills 1″ deep with 6 to 9″ between the rows. The seed, which is very small, is sprinkled thinly along the drill. The drills are best filled in by shuffling the soil into them with the feet and then treading it down using even pressure but avoiding digging in the heels.

The best months for sowing the seed are March, April and May so as to give a reasonable succession of crops.

When the resultant seedlings are large enough to handle – 4 to 6″ high – they are ready to be planted in the prepared beds. Plant them very firmly every 24″ in the rows which should be 30″ apart. Give a top dressing of a good general fertiliser when well established.

Harvesting

Harvest all shoots before any of the flowers start to open. Select broccoli which is fresh and clean with firm but tender stalks. The flower heads should be tightly closed in compact clusters with no yellow showing in the buds. 1½ lbs will provide 4 good servings.

Preparing

Wash well and trim the end of the stalk, but do not remove

the stems as the whole lot is edible. If the stems are more than 1″ in diameter they should be split up the middle.

Cooking

Drop the prepared broccoli into a small amount of salted, boiling water. Cover and cook for 10 to15 minutes, or until just tender.

Remove the spears from the water very carefully to avoid breaking the flower heads. Serve at once, seasoned with salt, pepper and melted butter or with hollandaise or cheese sauce.

Creamed Broccoli
Put ¾lb of cooked broccoli into1½ pints of medium white sauce. Heat thoroughly and serve.

Brussels Sprouts

Brussels sprouts are another member of the brassica family, so the same growing methods apply as for broccoli. They were first grown in the Belgian city of Brussels as long ago as the 13th Century, so it must be safe to say that it is a well established vegetable. There are many hybrid varieties available, so the original breeder would probably not recognise it now.

Growing

It is possible to grow different varieties to produce successive cropping from August through to March. To achieve this I would recommend the following three varieties: *peer gynt,* (early) with seed sown in a cold glasshouse in February and transplanted to a prepared bed later in March/early April, *prince askold* (mid-season) sown in seedbeds late March/early April and transplanted in May and finally, *fasolt* (late crop) with seeds sown in seedbeds in April and transplanted in May/June. Water and feed with liquid fertilizer during the growing season, especially in dry conditions.

Harvesting

Start cropping as soon as the bottom buttons are large enough (1″ in diameter). Do not remove the top of the plant until all the buttons are harvested This would cause the entire stem to mature together; good idea if you require the crop for freezing but not for successional cropping.

The tops, when harvested, can also be used as a vegetable.

1lb of Brussels sprouts are required for three servings. The buttons should be firm and resemble miniature cabbages. Blown sprouts are past their best. Sprouts should always be green in colour.

Preparing

Remove any loose or discoloured leaves. Trim the stem

end and wash thoroughly in cold water.

Cooking

Cook, covered in 1″ of boiling, salted water for 8 to 10 minutes, until tender.

Drain and serve at once, seasoned with pepper and melted butter.

Brussels sprouts can also be served with grated cheese, or in a medium white sauce as a creamed vegetable.

Deep Fried Brussels Sprouts
Cook the buttons as above. Dip in beaten egg and fine bread crumbs. Fry in hot fat until golden brown. Drain and serve after about 3 minutes.

Devilled Brussels Sprouts
Cook the sprouts and while cooking melt 3 table spoons of butter, add ¾ of a teaspoon of prepared mustard, a generous pinch of salt, ½ a teaspoon of Worcestershire sauce and a dash of cayenne pepper. Pour over the drained sprouts and serve.

Cabbage | Chinese

Chinese cabbage, sometimes called Chinese lettuce, or leaves, is a much closer relative to celery than to our usual cabbages and it has a much milder flavour than ordinary cabbage.

Growing

It requires ground preparation as for the brassicas, but the growing technique differs somewhat. Sow in June, directly into the cropping bed, very thickly in shallow drills. Just cover the seed with soil and have the rows 12″ apart. Thin the seedlings to 10″ apart.

Ensure that the plants do not lack moisture at any time.

Harvesting

Good, firm, solid heads will be ready in the autumn. Pick good, firm, crisp heads. 1lb of Chinese cabbage will give four servings.

Preparing

Wash thoroughly in cold water. The heads can either be cooked whole or shredded.

Cooking

To cook whole, cover with water in a saucepan and cook for 15 – 20 minutes. Shredded cabbage is cooked in 1½ pints of water. Cover the pan in both cases. Drain and serve with butter or a cream sauce.

Chinese cabbage can also be used raw, shredded in salads. The big outer leaf ribs may be cooked and served in the same way as asparagus.

Cabbage | Green

Cabbages are very easy crops to grow. There are many different varieties to choose from, depending on the time of year that the vegetable is required. There are spring heading cabbages, summer heading, autumn heading and winter heading ones, not forgetting the good old savoy cabbage.

Growing

Cabbages are all part of the brassica family so the usual growing procedures apply. According to the variety and the cropping period, the seeds are sown on seed beds in drills 1½″ deep from April until July.

When they are big enough, the plants are transferred to the prepared beds, 18″ between plants and rows. Spring heading varieties can be planted at 9″ intervals in the rows, so that every other one can be cut as spring greens when half grown.

Personally I would recommend the following varieties which should give continuous supplies throughout the year; *ormskirk savoy* for winter use, *wheeler's imperial* as a spring cabbage and greens, with *greyhound* for summer and early autumn crops followed by a *drumhead* for use in December.

Harvesting

Use cabbages that have reasonably solid heads and are heavy for their size.

Preparing

Wash well, cut into wedges and remove the core. They can be cooked as wedges or shredded.

Cooking

Put the wedges into a pot with 1" of boiling, salted water. Cover and cook for 10 to 15 minutes until just tender. Shredded cabbage is cooked uncovered in boiling, salted water for about 5 minutes. Drain and serve the cabbage at once, seasoned with pepper and butter.

Cabbage can also be eaten raw, finely shredded and incorporated into salads. Raw cabbage is very rich in vitamin C with a good content of vitamin B as well as many other essential minerals.

Cooking cabbage has a most notorious odour which can be decreased considerably by putting a complete, whole walnut in the cooking water.

Cabbage can be served creamed by heating cooked cabbage in either cream or a white sauce. For a novel touch, grated cheese and/or curry powder can be added to the sauce.

Sweet and Sour Cabbage

Shred a medium cabbage finely and season with salt and pepper. Peel and slice 3 small, sour apples. Melt 2 tablespoonsof fat in a pan, add the apple and cabbage, cover with boiling water and simmer until tender. Sprinkle with 2 tablespoons of flour, 3 tablespoons of lemon juice and 4 tablespoons of brown sugar. Simmer for another 10 minutes. Serve at once. (Serves 6)

Bavarian Cabbage

Sauté half a small, chopped onion in 1oz of bacon dripping or fat for five minutes. Add 1 tablespoon of vinegar, 1 tablespoon of brown sugar and mix it with 1lb of cooked cabbage. (Serves 4)

Buttered Cabbage

Cut a cabbage in half. Place the cabbage cut side down on a board and carefully slice it into thin segments. Do not remove the core as this will hold the segments together and stop them falling apart during cooking. Stand the segments in a saucepan just large enough to hold them upright. Sprinkle on a little salt and pepper and add a little butter. Pour ½"of boiling water into the pan and cover it. Bring to the boil, reduce the heat immediately and allow it to simmer for about 8 minutes. Drain well and serve onto the plate.

Cabbage | Greens

The term greens actually covers a very wide and varied list of crops. For the purpose of this book I will give a brief list of them but will concentrate on cabbage type greens and kales. Other greens that can be used are mainly the leaves or tops of other crops that are often discarded. They include young tender beetroot tops, carrot tops and turnip tops. These are all treated in the same manner as ordinary greens.

Growing

For greens, especially cabbage greens, the seeds are best sown thinly in drills 12″ apart on the site where you wish them to grow.

Harvesting

The greens are harvested straight from these rows when the plants are about half grown. Greens grown by this method are usually known as 'collards.' Alternatively, the plants can be transplanted at half-normal distance and cropped when well-grown, but before any heads form. This method is preferable for kale, which is gathered by removing the leaves and side shoots while young.

Choose greens that are crisp and tender, with a good, bright, fresh colour.

Preparing

Allow 1lb of greens for 4 servings.

Wash well and rinse three times for collard type greens. Strip out any coarse leaf ribs and discard. The greens can be cooked whole or shredded, according to preference.

Cooking

Cook covered with only the water that has clung to the greens for the rinsing. Boil until tender. Drain, chop or leave in sprays. Serve at once, seasoned with salt, pepper, butter and lemon juice.

Cabbage | Red

Red cabbage is grown in exactly the same way as green cabbage, with the seed sown in spring and transplanted when big enough. Red cabbage does not usually grow quite as big as green cabbage and, other than the colour, there is very little real difference.

Cooking

Follow directions and recipes as for green cabbage but add

the juice of a lemon to the cooking water to maintain the red colour of the cabbage. Serving suggestions are as for green cabbage.

Pickled Red Cabbage

Shred the cabbage finely. Pack it tightly into sealable jars, to within ½″ of lid. Fill the jars with spiced vinegar (boiled with pickling spice and allowed to cool). Seal tightly and store.

Red cabbage gives a nice bit of colour to a green salad. Shred finely and mix with green and white cabbage or lettuce.

Braised Red Cabbage

Cut a red cabbage into quarters, remove the outer leaves, white root and any other significant white pith. Shred the cabbage finely. Place it into a large bowl and cover it with boiling water. Leave for 1 minute and then drain.

Melt 2oz of butter or good bacon dripping into a large, heavy saucepan. Add 1 sliced, medium sized onion and cook it gently for about 5 minutes until it is soft but not brown. Add a large cooking apple, peeled, cored and thickly sliced, a ¼ pint of red wine or stock, salt, 1 tablespoon of vinegar, a few cloves, a ¼ teaspoon of grated nutmeg and plenty of black pepper. Add the cabbage and turn it over so that all the cabbage mixes into the liquid. Cover tightly and cook gently for about an hour, stirring occassionally, or until the cabbage is tender. Stir in 1 level teaspoon of soft brown sugar and serve.

Cabbage | White

White cabbage is grown in exactly the same way as any other cabbage.

Harvesting

White cabbage can be harvested in the autumn and stored in nets suspended from the roof of a frost free shed for winter use.

Preparing

Although white cabbage can be used in the same way as the other cabbages it is not often cooked, mainly because of the insipid colour attained through cooking. Only firm solid heads should be selected for use. Wash them well and shred finely.

Coleslaw

Remove the hard core from a small firm cabbage and shred the remainder very finely, adding 2 tablespoons of grated onion and 4oz of grated carrot to each pound of cabbage. Then chill the mixture. Blend 6 tablespoons of mayonnaise, 1 tablespoon of vinegar, 2 teaspoons of sugar and 1½ teaspoons of salt together and stir until the sugar has dissolved.

Carrots

Always a popular vegetable to grow, the root of the carrot is packed with vitamin A or carotene. Just 2oz of raw carrot provide the average daily requirement.

Carrots are a root crop and require a well prepared but not recently manured ground. Any garden should produce a reasonable crop of carrots provided that they are not very heavily shaded.

Growing

There are three types of carrot that can be grown, but these groupings only apply to the root shape and length of the growing period. They are the short-horn or stump rooted, the intermediate, and the long rooted. The seeds are thinly sown in drills 1½″ deep with 9″ between the rows for stump-rooted varieties and 12″ for the others.

Make the first sowings in March using a short-horn type and make successive sowings monthly until July. For main crop sowings using the intermediate and long rooted varieties are made in April. Thin the seedlings to 1″ apart as soon as they are big enough to handle.

Harvesting

When the roots are finger-sized, pull every other one for immediate use and allow the remaining ones to grow on.

Carrots should be brightly coloured with firm flesh.

The stump rooted varieties should be cropped as required. The main crop longer rooted types should be lifted in October, the tops twisted off and the roots stored in sand in a frost free shed, or they can be stored in a clamp outside. (Details for making a clamp are to be found at the end of this book)

Preparing

Remove any tops and scrape or peel thinly. Young carrots can be scrubbed with a stiff brush. Carrots can be used whole, sliced, diced or shredded.

Cooking

Cook covered in 1″ of boiling, salted water. Shredded carrots will need 5 minutes of gentle boiling, 10-15 minutes for cut roots and 15 to 20 minutes for whole carrots.

Candied Carrots.
Cut cooked carrots length wise into halves or quarters, depending on size. Melt 4oz of butter in a heavy pan, add 3oz of brown sugar and stir until melted. Add the carrots and cook until well glazed.

Carrot Mould
Blend together 1lb of mashed, cooked carrots, 2 teaspoons of finely chopped onion, 2 teaspoons of melted butter, 2 well beaten eggs, 1 teaspoon of flour and half a pint

of cream. Season to taste with salt, pepper and a pinch of paprika. Tightly pack the mixture into a greased ring mould. Place it in a shallow tray of hot water and bake it in a moderate oven (350°F gas mark 4) for 40-50 minutes. Serve the ring filled with green peas or beans, or it can be served with creamed chicken as a main course.

Carrot Soup

Melt 1oz of butter in a saucepan. Add some grated onion, 1lb of grated carrots and one finely chopped stick of celery and cook gently for about 10 minutes, allowing the vegetables to soften. Add 1 pint of stock and ½ a teaspoon of sugar, then simmer for 15 minutes.

Sieve, add the rest of the stock and test for seasoning. Bring it to the boil once more and stir in 2 tablespoons of single cream. Gently reheat and serve with sprinkled, chopped parsley.

Cauliflower

Cauliflowers are yet another member of the brassica family so the previous preparation rules prevail again.

Growing

For the earliest crops the seeds are best sown in a cold frame in September/October and overwintered there before planting out in a growing site during April. A second sowing can be made under heated glass in February, followed by further outdoor sowings in March, April and May to give successive cropping throughout the year.

The later sowings can be transplanted from April until August. Note that the late winter maturing varieties cannot be grown in exposed situations effectively. When the curds, or heads, start developing, some of the inner leaves should be bent over to cover them to keep them white. Suggested varieties for all the year round cultivation are *snowball* and the *roscoff* hybrids.

Harvesting

Cauliflowers should have bright leaves with a creamy, white, solid head. Yellowing leaves and/or a ricey looking curd means that the cauliflower is past its prime. Curd size is not important though, and neither are the small leaves that sometimes grow up through the head.

Preparing

Place the head downwards in cold water mixed with 1 teaspoon each of vinegar and salt. Soak for at least 10 minutes or up to an hour. This will refresh the head and remove any hidden worms. Remove the green stalks. The heads can be cooked whole or broken up into florets.

Cooking

Cook covered in 1˝ of salted, boiling water until tender.

Cauliflowers are best tested for tenderness by using a fork on the stem end. Florets need approx 10-12 minutes to cook. Double this time for whole heads. Serve hot with butter or, alternatively, serve with cheese sauce or hollandaise sauce.

Cauliflower can also be used raw. Break it up into florets and serve as a hors d'oeuvre with a dipping sauce, or incorporate it into a mixed vegetable salad.

Cauliflower à La Creole

Add 1 teaspoon of salt and a dash of black pepper to 8oz of canned or finely chopped fresh tomatoes. Cook until all the liquid has evaporated. Put 1lb of cauliflower florets into a greased casserole dish. Pour over the tomatoes and top it with 4oz of grated cheese mixed with 1oz of soft bread crumbs. Dot it with butter and bake slowly (325°F Gas mark 3) for 20 minutes. (Serves 4-5)

Celeriac

Celariac, sometimes referred to as celery root, grows with a bulbous root, visually not unlike a turnip. The seeds of celeriac are very small and resemble dust, so care must be taken to ensure that they are not sown too thickly.

Growing

The seed is sown in seedpans in a warm greenhouse in

late February/early March. The seedlings are pricked out, placed into deep boxes and hardened off ready for planting outdoors in late May/June.

This final planting should be on well dug and well manured ground. Take out a deep drill and plant the seedlings 9" apart in the bottom.

Celeriac produces best when given a plentiful supply of water. Once the plants are established a weekly feed of weak liquid manure will prove beneficial.

Harvesting

Lift as required when mature in late summer. Lift the remainder of the crop in late autumn before frosts begin and store in sand in a frost free shed.

Celeriac roots should be firm and solid. Half a pound of raw celeriac will yield 4 average servings.

Preparing

Remove all the leaves and any rootlets that may have developed. Scrub well but do not peel before cooking.

Cooking

Cook covered in boiling, salted water until tender. The

average cooking time is 45-55 minutes, depending on size. To serve, peel the cooked celeriac root, slice and serve hot with either melted butter, white or hollandaise sauce.

To serve celeric raw.
Peel, slice it very thinly and season it with salt, pepper and a little vinegar. Use as a relish.

Creamed Celeriac
Combine two cooked, sliced celeriac with ½ a pint of medium thickness white sauce. Serve it hot, garnished with parsley.

Celery

Celery is a wild plant that will grow practically everywhere and has done so for thousands of years. It had grown wild for many centuries before it was first cultivated as a domestic crop. It is generally agreed that the Italians can claim credit for this domestication. It is also accepted that celery was once known in England as 'smallage.'

Growing

Celery seed is sown in boxes in a heated greenhouse in March, with a further sowing in April to extend the growing season. When the seedlings are large enough to handle, prick out into boxes for growing on. Transplant them into well prepared cropping beds in May/June.

To prepare the cropping bed for celery dig deeply, incorporating plenty of manure or organic compost. Take out a trench 12-15″ wide and deep, incorporating more organic material in the base soil and refill two thirds of the trench. The top 5″ of the trench should not be refilled and the soil from there should be built up in ridges on each side of the trench. These ridges can be utilised during the early summer months by growing quick maturing crops such as lettuce or radishes on them. This is known as 'catch cropping.'

The celery plants are planted 12″ apart in the centre of the trench. Once the plants are established, feed them weekly with a weak liquid fertiliser. It is practically impossible to overwater celery during the growing season, so on no account allow the celery to dry out.

When the plants are approx 12″ high blanching can begin. This is best achieved by placing a 4″ collar of newspaper around the bottom of the plants. Draw some earth from the ridges around this collar and firm well.
Repeat this weekly until just a small tuft of leaves remain. It is advisable to sprinkle slug pellets along the trench as you earth up, as slugs can be a considerable pest with this crop.

Harvesting

The blanching usually takes 6-8 weeks and, after this time, the celery should be mature enough to begin harvesting. Dig up sufficient heads for immediate use, leaving the remainder in situ until required. Protect the heads in severe weather.

There is another type of celery that is self-blanching, both in name and habit. To grow this type which is only a summer crop, the seeds are planted as for ordinary celery and the culture is the same, except that instead of planting in rows, in trenches, self-blanching celery is grown in square blocks with the plants always 8-10˝ apart. Scaffolding boards can be placed along each side of these square beds to assist the blanching, but the plants effectively shade each other and so cause the stems to become a lighter colour.

Self-blanching celery is seldom as white as trench grown celery. There is also a red variety that is very late in maturing and can stand quite hard frosts.

The branches should be crisp with bright leaves on the ends.

Preparing

Remove all the leaves and trim off all the roots. Wash thoroughly using a brush to remove stubborn dirt. The outer branches are best used for dicing and cooking, while the more tender, thinner inner branches can be used raw.

Cooking

Cook diced celery in 1˝ of boiling, salted water for 15-20 minutes. Serve hot and seasoned with salt, pepper and melted butter or hollandaise sauce. Raw celery is served in sticks with salt or any preferred dipping sauces.

Creamed Celery

Mix 2 large bunches of celery, diced and cooked, to ½ a pint of medium thick white sauce. Serve hot. Chopped almonds can be sprinkled over the top and chopped, pre-cooked sweet peppers can also be added to the sauce. To turn this dish into celery au gratin simply place the above mixture in a heatproof dish, cover it with a layer of grated cheese and placeit under a hot grill until the cheese has melted and become a rich, golden brown. Serve at once.

Braised celery

Wash a head of celery thoroughly, removing all the leaves and cut it into 3″ pieces. Preheat 2 teaspoons of oil in a frying pan, add the celery and lightly brown it. Pour ½ a pint of meat stock or consommé type soup into the pan and simmer slowly until the liquid has reduced by half. Finally season with salt and pepper and serve hot.

Celery vinaigrette

Prepare and cook 1 head of celery cut into 8″ pieces until tender but not soft. Drain and let it get cold. Blend 4fl oz of cooking oil, 3fl oz of wine vinegar, 1 table spoon of chopped parsley, a quarter of a chopped onion and 2 tablespoons of chopped green peppers together. Season with salt and pepper.

Pour over the cold celery and place it in a refrigerator for at least 2 hours. Remove the celery from the marinade and serve. (Serves up to 5)

Chicory

Blanched heads of chicory are known as '*chicons*.' These plump, creamy white chicons provide a succulent and crisp salad vegetable during the winter. The chicons are actually young second growth shoots of the chicory plant.

Growing

Chicory will grow in any soil and on any site, provided it is not in heavy shade. Chicory seed is sown thinly in drills that are 12 to 15″ apart. The drills should be no deeper than half an inch.

A good way to make drills for chicory or, in fact, any other seed that needs shallow sowing, is to place a broom or rake handle along the drill line and lightly press it into the ground using your foot.
Sprinkle the seed as thinly as possible along this drill and cover it lightly with soil.

As soon as they are big enough to handle, thin out the seedlings to 6″ apart. Water them well and hoe around the plants regularly during the growing season.

Harvesting

Harvest in October or November when the leaves start to

turn yellow, but certainly before the frosts start. Lift the roots, twist off the leaves and cut or snap off the thin root end, leaving a plump, stubby root 8″ or so in length.

Pack these roots the right way up in sand, soil or well firmed peat in either deep boxes or large pots. Used seed or stale potting compost is an ideal medium for this purpose.

Place these filled boxes or pots in a warm cellar or a warm, dark and frost free shed. Under the bench in a warm greenhouse is also a good place to force chicory. Then cover the boxes or pots with another box or pot, making sure to exclude all light. In about 3 to 4 weeks the chicons will be ready for use.

To produce good chicons the temperature should be maintained at 50°F. Snap off blanched growths as close to the root as possible. To ensure a good succession, keep some prepared roots in frost free storage.

Preparing

Wash well. Large chicons can be halved lengthwise by cutting them with a sharp knife and starting at the root end.

Chicory chicons should be tight and creamy white in colour. They should also be tender but crisp. Chicory has a bitter but delicate flavour.

Cooking

To serve raw, you can use either whole chicons or they can be pulled apart for use in a mixed salad. Either way, serve with your favourite dressing.

Chicory with Egg and Lemon sauce

Take 4 large or 8 small chicons. If large heads are used, cut in them half lengthwise. Arrange the chicory in a large, heavy pan with any cut faces upwards.

Add ½ a pint of chicken stock, cover, bring to the boil and simmer until transparent and tender. This will take approximately 12 minutes. Take care not to over cook.

While the chicory is cooking, beat 2 egg whites until frothy but not stiff, add the egg yolks and continue beating until well blended. Add 2fl oz of lemon juice slowly while still beating and then continue beating until the mixture is thick and smooth.

Remove the cooked chicory from the pan and place it in a deep, pre-heated vegetable dish. Keep hot.

Measure the cooking liquid and make up to 6fl oz with boiling water if necessary. Slowly pour the hot liquid into the egg mixture, stirring the whole time. Return it to the pan and cook until thickened, over a low heat, stirring constantly.

When the sauce has thickened, pour over the chicory.

Garnish with watercress or parsley and serve immediately. (Serves 4)

Corn

Maize, corn on the cob, sweet corn, or Indian corn (call it what you will) is yet another vegetable that has a noteworthy history of cultivation. It was being grown by the Peruvian indians when the first Spanish settlers arrived in South America, hence the name 'Indian Corn.' At that time the kernels were red, white, yellow and even black, all in the same ear, but through careful, scientific breeding over the years the modern yellow hybrids that we know as sweet corn were developed. When the crop is grown as maize it is often harvested before the ears have developed fully and is then made into silage for the winter feeding of livestock. Alternatively, it is also grown on and the resultant crop of ripe kernels used to make cornflakes.

Growing

Good, well prepared and manure enriched soil in a sunny location is ideal for growing corn. Plant the seeds ¼" deep in peat pots in a temperature of 50°F in April.

Plant it out in the cropping area in June with 15" between plants and a row width of 24". It is better to plant in square blocks rather than in straight rows. This is because each plant carries both male and female flowers separately on each plant. The mail tassels release pollen which floats on the wind to be collected by the silks, or hairs, on the female embryo ear.

Block planting allows the wind to achieve this more effectively. Seeds can also be sown direct in mid May, with 2-3 seeds at each station, ultimately being thinned to 1 only. Begin gathering the ears in August.

Harvesting

The ears are ready for use if the kernels emit a milky fluid when punctured. There should be no spaces between the kernels. The husks should be green and look fresh. The ears should be well filled with tender kernels. Small, soft kernels indicate that the ears are immature.

Preparing

Wash and remove both husks and silk immediately prior to using.

Cooking

Corn on the Cob

Line the bottom of a large pan with some of the husks. Put in the corn cobs and cover them with unsalted, boiling water. Cover the pan and cook for about 5 minutes. To serve, lift the corn from the water, drain and serve hot with salt, pepper and plenty of butter. Don't forget the napkins!

Mexican Sweet Corn Custard

Remove the kernels from about 8 cobs. This amount should provide roughly 14oz of kernels.

Cook 1oz of chopped onion with 1oz of chopped green pepper in a little melted butter for 3 minutes. Add 3 table spoons of chopped pimentos and mix with the corn. Slightly beat 2 eggs, add 1 teaspoon of sugar and 1 pint of hot milk. Mix in the corn and pimentos and season with salt and pepper. Pour into a well greased 2½ pint casserole. Place in a pan of hot water and bake in a slow oven (325°F Gas mark 3) for 75 minutes or until a clean knife inerted into the centre remains clean when withdrawn. (Serves 6)

Sweet Corn can be roasted by placing the ears, still in their husks, into a hot oven and baking for about 15 minutes, or until the corn is tender. Creamed sweet corn is made by adding the cooked kernels to a white sauce.

Cucumbers

There are two types of cucumber in general cultivation. One is the long, smooth skinned type that is sold in shops and is cultivated under glass. The second type is the ridged cucumber which is grown outdoors and is stubby and rough skinned.

Growing

Indoor cucumbers can be grown all year round, provided

a heated greenhouse is available. Otherwise the crop can only be grown in a cold house during the summer.

The seeds of all cucumbers are sown individually in 3″pots. The earliest sowings for indoor cropping can begin in January and continue through to late April, at reasonable intervals. Outdoor varieties are sown in one batch in late April.

The new all female F1 hybrids are the best varieties to choose for indoor cultivation as they eliminate the problem of male flowers having to be removed throughout the growing season so as to avoid fertilisation, which causes the fruit to become bitter and bulbous in shape.

All cucumbers need rich soil so site preparation is very important. indoor cucumbers are planted into their growing beds when about 6″ high. I prefer to plant them along a ridge made up of soil and well rotted compost, but it is quite in order to plant on the level ground. As the plants grow they will need tying for support. Some growers have a series of horizontal wires to which they tie the growth as it appears. I prefer just one wire about 7ft high, a method I find also works for tomatoes. As soon as the plants are planted out and established, I tie a loose loop of soft, strong string around the stem of the plants, the other end being tied to the high wire by a couple of turns and a half hitch so that it can be easily untied for adjustment. The main plant stem is made to curl up and around this string in a clockwise direction. Most climbing plants readily follow the sun when growing. When the growing tip reaches the wire it is pinched out. All laterals from the main stem are stopped at 2 leaves and allowed to hang loose.

Ridge cucumbers are planted on ridges or mounds in a similar fashion but are allowed to run, only being stopped to keep them within bounds. Do not remove the male flowers from ridge plants as fertilisation is necessary for the fruits to develop. Gherkin for pickling are grown in the same way as ridge cucumbers.

Harvesting

Cut the fruit as and when it is ready. Cutting as soon as it is a useable size encourages further development. Firm, fresh cucumbers are bright green in colour and the colour is important as dark green or yellowish fruits are past their best.

Preparing

To serve raw there is no need to peel the cucumber unless the skin is very tough. For cooking the cucumbers should be peeled thinly and cut into thick slices.

Cooking

Peel and slice the cucumbers thickly. Marinate them in vinegar seasoned with salt, pepper and a finely sliced onion.

Lightly cooked

Cook in a small amount of boiling salted water for about 10-12 minutes until tender. Serve hot with melted butter and pepper.

Sautéed Cucumbers

Peel and cut the cucumber into 4″ slices. Dry them on paper towels, dip them into seasoned flour and fry in melted butter until golden. Drain and Serve

Baked, Stuffed Cucumbers

Wash 4 large cucumbers. Cut in half lengthways. Remove the seed portion without damaging the remaining fleshy part, then parboil the cucumber shells in slightly salted water for 10 minutes. Then drain them.

Cook half a small chopped onion and 2 table spoons of chopped parsley in 1oz of butter. Add 4oz of fine bread crumbs, 8fl oz of tomato pulp and the cucumber pulp. Season with salt and pepper and cook for 5 minutes.

Fill the cucumber shells with the hot stuffing, place them in a shallow baking dish with enough water to stop them sticking and bake in a moderate oven (350°F Gas mark 4) for 15 minutes until the stuffing is golden brown on top.

Dandelion

It is often a topic of argument whether dandelion is a herb

or a vegetable. The cultivated variety has been bred to produce larger leaves than the wild (or weed) dandelion, although botanically they are the same. They prefer a moist, fertile soil in a shady situation to produce large leaves.

Growing

Seeds are sown in April and the plants thinned to 6″ apart. Somewhat ironically you must keep them weed free.

Harvesting

The roots may be harvested in October. If the leaves are required for salads, cover the crowns with boxes in the following spring to produce blanched leaves. The leaves can be used as a green vegetable and are prepared as for ordinary greens. Dandelion leaves should be fairly large but tender and have a fresh green appearance.

Preparing

Wash the leaves well. Scrub the roots and trim off any rootlets.

Cooking

Dandelion roots should be roasted until thoroughly dried and shrivelled. When cold, the roots can be ground up finely and used as an additive to coffee or indeed as a coffee substitute. Dandelion leaves are cooked in the same way as cabbage greens.

Dandelion Salad.
Take ½lb of young dandelion leaves. Wash, dry and chop them coarsely. Add 4 thinly sliced spring onions and mix lightly with French dressing. Place them in a salad bowl and garnish with thinly sliced tomatoes. Serve chilled.

Endive

There are two types of endive available; the Batavian broadleaf variety resembles a cos lettuce in appearance and the curled type which has divided curled leaves. It is the Batavian endive that is often sold by the greengrocer as Escarole. All varieties of endive are members of the same family as chicory, although the growing habits do differ.

Growing

All garden sites with well cultivated soil are suitable for growing endive. The seeds of the curled endive are sown from late April until June and the Batavian variety is sown from June to August as it is more hardy and will last well into the winter if given some protection with cloches. The seeds of both varieties are sown in drills ½" deep with the rows 12-15" apart on the site where you want the plants to crop.

As soon as the seedlings are big enough to handle, thin them down to 9" apart. Keep weeds under control with regular hoeing and apply a top dressing or liquid feed of a nitrogenous fertilizer to encourage rapid growth.

When the plants are well developed, cover them with an inverted large flower pot with the drainage hole covered so as to exclude all light in order to blanch the leaves.

Harvesting

Blanching should take about 6 weeks, after which the endive will be ready for use. Later winter crops can be covered with black polythene to both blanch and protect the plants. In order to harvest the centres of the heads should be a yellowish white.

Preparing

Wash well and remove any outer leaves of a darker colour as they are inclined to be bitter. If the hearts are not as white as desired, leave them overnight under a damp cloth.

Cooking

Endive is usually used raw in salads. The leaves can be used either whole or can be shredded according to preference. It can also be braised and served as a hot vegetable, as which it can be quite delicious.

Braised Endive

Wash 4 heads of endive thoroughly. Blanch them in boiling water for 10 minutes. Drain, cut in half and place them in a greased, oven proof dish. Add 3 tablespoons of lemon juice, 4fl oz of chicken stock, 1 tablespoon of sugar and ½oz of butter.

Bring to the boil and simmer gently for 25 minutes. Remove the endive into a heated vegetable dish. Reduce the liquid. Blend a knob of butter with 1 tablespoon of flour and stir into the liquid, a little at a time. Pour the thickened liquid over the endive and serve at once.

Fennel

There are two varieties of fennel grown in the kitchen garden. One is the common fennel which is a perennial herb. The other variety has similar leaves but is grown for bulbous swelling of the leafbases. This is known as Florence fennel or finocchio. It is with this second variety that we are concerned here.

Growing

Florence fennel is best grown on well drained soil in a sunny position. The seeds are sown directly into the cropping bed in shallow drills with rows 18″ apart. As soon as the seedlings are of handling size, thin them to 10″ between plants. Keep weed free and as the leaf bases begin to swell, draw the soil up around them to blanch them white.

Harvesting

Harvest them when well developed, lifting as required. The bulbs should be both well developed and tender.

Preparing

Scrape the bulbs and cut both the bulbs and stalk into 1″ slices.

Cooking

Cook them covered in a small amount of salted, boiling water until just tender (15-20 minutes). Serve hot seasoned with salt, pepper, melted butter and fresh lemon juice.

To serve raw fennel should be sliced very thinly and used in salads where it can be treated similar to celery.

Baked Fennel

Take 1 whole fennel bulb for each person. Remove any coarse outside leaves and cook in salted, boiling water until tender for about 20 minutes. Cut vertically into 4 slices and arrange in an oven proof dish with melted butter (½oz per bulb). Pour 1 tablespoon of milk per bulb over the fennel. Sprinkle with grated cheese and dot with more butter. Bake in a moderate oven (400° F Gas Mark 6) until golden brown (about 20 minutes).

Garlic

Garlic, also known as clove garlic, originates from Central Asia and is one of the oldest recorded plants. It was in Greek legend that Odysseus is said to have used moly, a wild garlic, as a charm to keep the sorceress, Circe, from transforming him into a pig. The Egyptians used it medicinally. It is said that all the slaves building the pyramid of Cheops were each given a garlic clove every day to sustain their strength, as were the Roman army. It was probably the Roman army which invaded Britain that brought it here.

During the first world war spaghnum moss was soaked in garlic juice and used as an antiseptic wound dressing.

Garlic is a hardy perennial plant that is usually grown as an annual. A clove of garlic is a bulb made up of several smaller bulbs, all encased in a white, papery skin. These cloves are usually a light pink in colour, although they can vary from white to a dark pink. Garlic usually has green leaves. It rarely flowers in this country but if it does the flowers have round heads and vary in colour from white to pink.

Growing

Plant the individual cloves outdoors directly into the soil. Plant them in full sun in a rich, light soil from autumn through to spring. Traditionally garlic cloves are best planted on the shortest day and harvested on the longest day.

They will be well matured in the summer when the tops start changing colour and keel over. Some schools of thought state that tying the foliage into a knot will increase the size of the resultant crop.

Harvesting

Ease the bulbs out of the soil when the leaves are down and have lost their greenness. Allow them to dry in the sun for a few days but remove them indoors if there is rain about. When dry, hang them up in a net bag or plait them into a string. Store the where it is cool and airy.

Cooking

Garlic is a very pungent culinary herb. The flavour is lively in the early spring but from late spring onwards the cloves should be cleaned by removing the green filaments and the outer skin to make it more digestible.

Whole cloves can be split into individual segments and roasted under a leg of lamb or sliced into slivers and place just under the surface of the meat. The longer that the garlic is cooked, the milder it becomes.

A peeled clove can be left to stand in a vinaigrette but it must be removed before dressing a salad. Alternatively, rub the cut surface of a clove around the salad bowl.

It has been suggested that garlic, when planted under a fruit tree, especially peach, will ward off leaf curl. It is also thought that when used as a companion plant with roses it wards off black spot.

Garlic juice is said to be good for repelling flying insects and neutralizes the poisons of their bites and stings. It is also a wonderful glue and, when a clove is crushed, rubbed onto glass and allowed to dry, you can cut or drill a hole cleanly into the glass.

Horseradish

Horseradish is a hardy perennial. It is also the perfect accompaniment for roast beef. A native of Europe , it has now been naturalised in this country although it rarely flowers here. When it does flower it produces white flowers in spring. The foliage consists of large, oblong shaped leaves and the root, which can be 24″ long and 2″ thick, is tapered and goes down deep into the soil.

Growing

Take root cuttings in early spring by selecting 6″ long pieces of root about ½″ thick. Plant them outside directly into the cropping area at a depth of 2″ and 12″ apart. The earlier this is done, the better.

Maintain the soil well as any cuttings will take about three years to grow to maturity. Although horseradish will grow in impoverished soils it really does appreciate a light, well dug, rich, moist soil.

Spray plants with a general purpose liquid fertiliser about once a fortnight during the summer.

Harvesting

Collect the leaves while young for used either fresh or dried. Dig up mature roots (3 years old) and store them in sand in a dark, frost free place for the winter. It is also possible to wash, slice and dry the roots, but doing this has been known to reduce a man to tears so you have been warned! Freeze and/or grate as required.

Potatoes are said to be more resistant to disease if horseradish is grown near by. Do not allow the horseradish to get a hold or else it will take over just about everything else that you are trying to grow.

Cooking

As a cooked vegetable the root of the horseradish is useless as all the taste of the volatile oils that give the plant its flavour are lost during the cooking process. In its raw state, however, the roots come into their own as they can be used in sauces, vinegars and as an addition to coleslaw, dips, pickled beet, cream cheese, mayonnaise, mashed potato and even for the filling of an avocado.

The spring root is fairly mild. It is in the autumn that the richest flavours will be obtained. Horseradish roots that are chopped very finely and added to dog food will get rid of any worms and will improve body tone. Sprayed onto fruit trees, especially apple, horseradish will control brown rot. Simply take a pint of warm water, grate into it 1oz of horseradish. Stir well, dilute 4:1 and spray away!.

As a warning, too much usage may result in skin blistering. Do not use it if you have low thyroid functions or if you are on thyroxin. Also control the amount of usage when pregnant or suffering with any kidney disease.

Horseradish Sauce

Grate 4 tablespoons of horseradish and mix it with 1 teaspoon of English mustard (optional), 2 tablespoons of white wine vinegar, salt, pepper and ¼ pint of double cream. Blend them together and put in the fridge to set.

Horseradish butter

Quantities for this are very much according to taste, so please regard the recipe as a method only. Cream some butter, a teaspoon of mustard, some grated horseradish and black pepper together. This creation will add real zing to a humble corn on the cob.

Kale

Kale, or borecole as it is sometimes called, is a large and hardy curly leafed member of the cabbage family that is used as a winter vegetable. Details on the cultivation of kale have already been dealt with under the heading 'cabbage; greens.'

Harvesting

Choose kale that is dark green in colour. Leaves with a slight brown tinge around the edges can be trimmed for use.

Preparing

Cut off any roots or stalk and wash very thoroughly. Remove any hard, coarse ribs from the leaves and trim any brown edges.

Cooking

For each pound of prepared kale, add ½ a pint of water with a ½ teaspoon of salt. Bring this to the boil and cover and cook for 15-20 minutes until tender. Drain, chop and add a little melted butter with a dash of lemon juice. Mix it all together and top with a chopped, hard boiled egg and serve. Kale can also be creamed by replacing the butter and lemon juice with 6oz of medium white sauce.

Country Style Kale

Cook the kale as above. Drain, chop and return it to the saucepan. To each pound of raw kale, add 3 tablespoons of bacon fat and 1 tablespoon of pickle relish. Heat well and serve hot.

Kohl Rabi

Kohl rabi is another member of the cabbage family with a thick, turnip shaped bulb. The bulbs are used as a vegetable and the young, tender leaves can be eaten as greens.

Growing

Kohl rabi can be grown in any reasonably well cultivated soil provided that it is not too dry or shady. Thinly sow three batches of seed from April to August on the cropping site in shallow drills with the rows 12″ apart. Thin the seedlings to 10″ apart in the rows as soon as practical. If the soil is inclined to acidity or has been used extensively for growing members of the brassica family, dust the soil with lime before sowing. Hoe regularly to control weeds and water well in dry weather with occasional liquid feeds.

Preparing

Remove the leaves and peel thinly, either slicing or cubing the bulbs.

Cooking

Cook covered in a small amount of salted, boiling water until tender. This should require about 25 minutes.

Serve hot with pepper and melted butter or as a creamed vegetable in a medium white sauce. Kohl rabi can also be served with boiled chestnuts or grilled mushrooms. A topping of grated nuts is another delicious way of serving this vegetable. Try mashing the cooked bulbs seasoned with salt and pepper and shape them into patties. Dip them in seasoned flour and fry until golden brown. Scrumptious!

Leeks

Leeks are a mild flavoured member of the onion family and are often served alone as a vegetable. They are also often combined with other ingredients in a variety of dishes.

Growing

Leeks require deep, rich and well cultivated soil to produce their best offerings. Seeds can be sown in boxes in a warm greenhouse during January/February for early crops. Otherwise they are sown in a seed bed in March/April for a later cropping.

Leek seeds are sown thinly in shallow drills 1ft apart and transplanted to the cropping site. The early raised plants should be ready for this move in May, followed in June by the later sowings. The ideal size for transplanting is when the plants are approximately pencil sized. To transplant leeks, take a dibber and make holes 9″ apart, 6-8″ deep in rows 18″ apart. Drop 1 plant into each hole and water it in. Do not fill in the holes. The plants will do this as they grow.

Water them well in dry conditions using a dilute liquid fertilizer. As the plants grow, draw the earth up around them while hoeing. In the later stages of growth, trim back the big, old leaves by half as this will encourage a larger white stem. Leeks will be ready for cropping when the stems are 1-1½″ in diameter. Dig as and when required. It is a good idea to give some protection to the later crop during bad winter weather.

Preparing

Trim off all the leaves within two inches of the white stem. Wash well. To thoroughly clean larger leeks it can be advisable to split the stem from the leaf end for two thirds of its length, before running fresh water through it.

Cooking

Cook for about 15 minutes covered in boiling, salted water until just tender. Serve hot, seasoned with pepper and melted butter. Leeks can also be served creamed in a medium white sauce.

Leeks au Gratin
Arrange cooked stalks in a baking dish and season with salt and pepper. Sprinkle with grated cheese and place under a hot grill until the cheese melts to a golden brown. Serve

immediately.

Carrot and Leek Soup

Thinly slice 2 carrots and 2 leeks. Sauté them in 1oz of butter for 7 minutes, then add 1 teaspoon of horseradish sauce, 1oz of medium oatmeal, salt, pepper, 1 teaspoon of mace and a bayleaf. You can also add a cinnamon stick.

Add 1 pint of stock and ¼ pint of milk and bring to the boil. Allow it to simmer for 25 minutes and then blend, remembering to remove the bayleaf and cinnamon stick beforehand.

Cawl Cennin (Leek Broth)

This Cawl, or broth, was nearly always made whenever a piece of Bacon was cooked and would be used as a first course or kept for another meal. The oatmeal is optional and can be left out if a thinner broth is required.

Put 8oz of potatoes and 8oz of carrots (both peeled and diced) into 1½ pints of stock and bring to the boil. Keep on the boil for 10 minutes. Add 2 large, sliced leeks and half a finely shredded cabbage.

Mix 2 tablespoons of oatmeal and a little cold water together. Add them to the broth. Bring it to the boil once again and allow it to simmer for 15 minutes or until all the vegetables are cooked and tender. Check the seasonings and serve garnished with chopped parsley.

Lettuce

There are two main types of lettuce, but there are a great many varieties within these two groups, giving differences in colour, shape, texture, size and cropping seasons. With protection it is possible, when combined with a good selection of varieties, to crop lettuce for most of the year. Catalogues from the seedsmen are always a great help in giving advice on varieties to use for a good succession, usually with the use of detailed cropping charts.

Growing

Lettuces like a rich, well dug and well manured soil. They are often used as catch crops on the ridges of celery trenches and between the rows of crops that take longer to grow and mature.

Sowings for the earliest crops are sown in boxes of sandy soil under glass in February, with the seedlings being pricked out into other boxes as soon as they can be handled, before being grown on and hardened off ready for transplanting in the cropping beds in April.

Other sowings are made outside at fortnightly intervals from March to September according to variety and cropping period. The seed is sown thinly in shallow drills 12″ apart with the resultant seedlings being thinned out to every 9″.

Some gardeners advocate transplanting these thinnings, but I don't agree as they never seem to do as well as the untransplanted ones, especially in hot or dry summers. The only exception to this is the September sowings which should be planted out in a sheltered site where cloches can be used to cover some of them. Other September sown varieties are available for planting out under glass for winter cultivation.

Harvesting

Choose a lettuce that feels heavy for its size, with clean leaves free from rusty looking, burn like marks.

Preparing

Thoroughly wash and shake dry after removing any roots or coarse outer leaves. Lettuce leaves can be used whole, halved or shredded depending whether they are being used as a garnish, a bed for other dishes or as an ingredient in a salad.

Cooking

In this country lettuce is very rarely cooked. It is more commonly used as a base for salad making or as a bed of green for other dishes. On the Continent, however, lettuce is often cooked, mainly by braising.

Braised Lettuce (French style).

Take 1 large lettuce heart and cut it into quarters. Soak the lettuce in cold water for one hour. Drain and tie each quarter together firmly with string. Cook in boiling, salted water for 10 minutes. Drain and remove the string.

Melt 2 tablespoons of butter in a heavy frying pan, add the lettuce and season with salt, pepper and a pinch of nutmeg, then cook slowly for another 35 minutes. Pour 1 tablespoon of lemon juice over the lettuce and serve. (Serves 3)

Mushrooms

Mushrooms have never really have been a crop for the kitchen garden, except on big estates where the gardens were labour intensive. This was because tons of good quality stable manure had to be composted down by turning sides to middle and top to bottom several times before the compost was ready for use. Once the compost was ready it had to be packed in deep mushroom trays, allowed to heat up again and then, as it cooled, spawning took place. Cropping would hopefully start in six to twelve weeks after spawning. The whole job, from start to cropping, would take about 4 – 5 months with a great deal of really hard work involved.

Growing

Happily nowadays there is a way of growing mushrooms on

a small scale that is a lot easier and cleaner as well as being much quicker. All good seedsmen now carry mushroom growing kits in their stocks so they are easy to obtain. All you have to do is place the container where you wish to grow your crop of mushrooms, remove the top, water and await your crop. Complete full intructions come with the kits so you cannot go wrong.

If, however, you would like to try the old fashioned way, it is still possible to do so. Purchase 4 large bales of straw and break them open. Shake all the straw loose and soak them thoroughly with warm water. Put down a layer of wet straw on a firm base, making it about 3ft wide, 6ft long and 6″ deep. Sprinkle a liberal amount of sulphate of ammonia over this layer and tread it down firmly. Spread another layer on top and continue until all the straw is used. Cover the stack and leave it.

In about a week to 10 days uncover the stack and turn the entire heap over, ensuring that the outsides change places with the middle. As you rebuild the heap make sure that you keep treading the straw firmly down, watering any dry places as you do so. Cover the heap once more. Repeat this process a further 3 – 4 times until the straw becomes a free-flowing, crumbly compost.

When you have reached this stage it is time to make your beds up. Wooden trays 30″ wide by 60″ long and 6″ deep are ideal. Pack the compost tightly into these boxes and cover. Allow the bed to heat up and start to cool down again. Now is the time to spawn the beds. Break up the blocks of mushroom spawn into walnut size pieces. Insert 1 piece of spawn every 9″ each way about 1-2″ deep. Lightly water the beds and cover. In 10 days time check the spawn and you should see white threads growing from it. If so, completely cover the beds with 2″ of sterilized, moist soil, packed down tightly. Water and cover with dry straw.

Harvesting

With luck your first mushrooms will appear in about another 3-4 weeks. Pick them daily as soon as they are a nice button size by twisting the mushrooms from the bed.

It is best to grow mushrooms in the dark, but it is not absolutely essential. You should crop about 50lbs of mushrooms from this amount of compost and afterwards you will still have the spent compost for use on your other plots.

The mushrooms should be firm, white to creamy white but without any blemishes.

Preparing

Clean by brushing lightly. Do not wash mushrooms unless they are very dirty. If you do need to wash them, do it very quickly without allowing them to soak in water. There should not be any need to peel fresh, cultivated mushrooms. Leave them whole or remove the stems and chop them up, leaving the cups whole.

Cooking

There are many different ways of cooking mushrooms and there are literally hundreds of dishes prepared where the mushroom is used as an ingredient, but here I am concentrating on mushrooms as a vegetable.

Sautéed Mushrooms
Cook them covered in a frying pan in 2oz of melted butter for 8-10 minutes. Season with salt and pepper. Serve as a hot vegetable. They can be combined with other hot, cooked vegetables such as peas, beans or corn.

Creamed Mushrooms
Cook as for sautéed mushrooms but blend in 1 tablespoon of flour per lb of mushrooms. Cook for 5 minutes. Add 1 pint of single cream and complete the cooking time. Serve immediately.

Grilled Mushrooms
Clean the mushrooms and remove the stems. Chop them up and season with salt and pepper. Grill the cups with the gills face down for 3 minutes under a moderate grill. Turn and season. Fill the cups with the chopped stems and dot with butter. Grill for another 3 minutes. Serve on toast, taking care not to lose any juices when removing them from the grill pan.

Mushrooms Baked in Cream
Remove the stems from some cleaned, large mushrooms. Place them in a shallow, greased baking dish with the gills

uppermost. Season with salt and pepper. Dot with butter. Pour single cream around them and cook in a very hot oven (450°F Gas mark 8) for 10 minutes. Serve on dry toast, pouring the remaining hot cream over the top.

Stuffed Mushrooms

Remove the stems from some large cup mushrooms. Fill the hollow with a mixture of 3oz of cooked sausage meat, blended with 2 tablespoons of red wine and a dash of paprika pepper. Grill them until tender. Serve hot on cocktail sticks. The above mixture would stuff 8 medium to large mushrooms.

Mushrooms can also be stuffed using chopped ham in a thick cream sauce or crabmeat in thick cream and mushrooms grilled with strong cheddar cheese and served hot are a pleasant variation to grilled mushrooms. Try using goats cheese too, either the soft or the hard variety.

All cultivated mushrooms are safe to eat, but avoid any wild ones unless you have been properly trained or have a very good identification aid to hand because, although many of them look like the cultivated ones, they are, on occasion, deadly poisonous to humans.

Mushroom Soup

Melt 1oz of butter in a heavy based saucepan which has a lid. Fry one large onion, 1oz of finely chopped green pepper and a crushed clove of garlic until soft, but not brown. Add 4oz of mushrooms and toss them together over a low heat. Add salt and pepper, taking care not to over salt if the stock you will be using is well seasoned. Put the lid on and let the contents sweat over a low heat for 5 or 10 minutes. If you are using old mushrooms, 5 minutes is plenty. Do not let them catch. Stir in 2 spoons of flour, add ¾ pint of chicken stock and bring to the boil. Simmer for 5 minutes. (You can freeze it at this point). Prior to serving, add ¾ pint of milk and gently reheat.

Onions

There are several different varieties of onion that can be grown. Some are entirely round while others can be both flat and round. These varieties, including the Spanish onion, are all known as 'domestic onions.' Onions over 1½" in diameter are sometimes called boilers, while the smaller ones can be known as picklers.

Growing

Onions are undoubtedly one of the easiest crops to grow. They can be grown from seed, but it is far quicker and easier to use onion sets. These are very young onions that have been grown from seed but have had their growth stopped at an early stage. You can simply plant the sets 6" apart in rows 12-15" wide in well prepared and rich soil.

Each set is pushed firmly into place and left to resume growth. A few days after planting the sets it is a good idea to check on them as birds sometimes decide to pull them up. Keep clear of weeds and water well in dry spells.

Plant the sets in March/April and wait to harvest the bulbs in September.

Some bulbs may be pulled as required for immediate use during the growing period but the majority should be allowed to mature fully in order to store them for winter and spring use. As growth slows down in late summer, bend over any tops that have not done so naturally. This helps to form a better bulb.

Harvesting

When fully developed, the onions are lifted and left to ripen in the sun. Cover the bulbs for protection in wet weather. When fully dried and ripe, collect the bulbs and store them in a dry, frost free place.

Good onions should be well shaped with thin necks and bright, hard bulbs. The skin should be dry enough to crackle when rubbed. When onions are being used as a main vegetable, allow 6oz of raw onion per portion.

Preparing

You must, of course, peel them. Tears caused by the peeling of onions can be avoided if boiling water is poured over the bulbs, which are then immediately plunged into cold water. The skin will then simply slip off.

Cooking

Place whole, peeled onions into boiling, salted water. Cook them for 20 to 30 minutes, according to size. Drain and serve hot with salt, pepper and melted butter or with a medium thick white sauce.

Sautéed Onions.
Peel and thickly slice several large onions. Melt 3 tablepoons of butter or oil in a pan with a tight fitting lid. Add the onion slices and season them with salt and pepper to taste. Cover and cook them for 20 minutes or until tender. Serve hot, sprinkled with chopped parsley.

Grilled onions
Grill several thick slices of onion in a greased, shallow pan until tender, turning once.

Stuffed Onions
Skin the onions, leaving the root end on the base of the bulbs. Partly cook them in boiling, salted water. Drain and remove a thin slice from the top of each bulb and remove the centre to leave a shell.

While the onions are cooking, the stuffing can be prepared by lightly sautéeing half a chopped green pepper with 8oz of diced mushrooms. Add 8oz of cooked rice. Also chop up the parts of the onions you have removed and mix them with the stuffing.

Fill the onion cases and cover the tops with a mixture of grated cheese and breadcrumbs. Dot with butter and place in a little water in a shallow oven dish. Bake in a moderate oven (375° F Gas mark 5) for 15 minutes or until golden brown. (Serves 6)

Deep Fried Onion Rings

Slice some prepared onions into 1½" slices and separate them into rings. Dip the rings into some seasoned milk and seasoned breadcrumbs. Deep fry them in very hot fat for about 3 minutes until golden brown. Drain and serve.

Onions can also be baked in cream using the recipe for the same mushroom dish, but substituting thin onion slices instead of mushrooms.

Onion Soup

Melt 2oz of butter in a large saucepan, add 1½lb of chopped onion and lightly fry until soft. Add 1 level tablespoon of flour and seasoning and cook for 2 minutes, stirring continuously. Finally, stir in 2 pints of stock and bring to the boil. Allow it to simmer for 30 minutes.

Cheese and Onion Savoury

Peel and thinly slice 1lb of onions. Place them in a saucepan with ½ a teaspoon of salt and just enough milk to cover the onions. Cook gently until the onions are soft and put them in a shallow casserole dish.

Cover with thinly sliced cheese. Sprinkle over 2 tablespoons of fresh breadcrumbs with a dash of black pepper. Arrange thickly sliced tomatoes along the centre of the dish and dot with butter. Place in a pre-heated oven (350°F Gas mark 4) and leave until all the cheese melts. Serve at once with a thick slice of bread to mop up the juices.

Onions | Spring

Spring onions, salad onions, scallions or chippoes are all different names, depending on the locality, for pencil thick, undeveloped onions that are mainly used raw as a salad vegetable. They can be cooked and are quite often used in Chinese style stir fry dishes.

Growing

Spring onions like a rich, well cultivated soil. The seed is sown in shallow drills with rows 6″ apart. Sowings made monthly from March to September will provide good crops of spring onions the whole year round.

Harvesting

Spring onions should have crisp green tops with pencil thick 2-3″ white stems. Allow 6-8 for each portion.

Preparing

Wash them well. Trim off the roots and tops and remove any loose layers of skin.

Cooking

Cook in a small amount of salted, boiling water for 8 to 10 minutes or chop and cook them mixed with other vegetables. Serve with freshly ground pepper and butter. To serve raw prepare as above and serve whole and crisp with a dipping sauce or chop them up to mix in salads.

Onions | Welsh

Sometimes called the Japanese Leek, these are evergreen, hardy perennials. The leaves are green, hollow, tubelike cylinders. Flowers are produced on the second year's growth and are a greenish yellow in colour. It orginates from Siberia.

The origin of this plant is uncharted as it effectively predates both history and historians. It was probably introduced to Europe by the Romans. In the Middle Ages it was believed that a bunch of onions hung outside a door would prevent infection by the plague. It was widely recognised as a strong disinfectant, mainly because of its sulphur content. The juice of this onion has also been used to heal both gunshot and gunpowder wounds.

Growing

Welsh Onion seeds lose their viability within two years, so it is advisable to sow the seeds almost as soon as collected. Sow them in either late winter or early spring under cover with a bottom heat of 65°F (18°C). Cover them with vermiculum or perlite. When the seedlings are big enough, and after having hardened them off, they should be planted out into a prepared bed at a distance of 9" apart.

Each year the Welsh onion will produce big clumps of onions, so every third year they should be lifted, separated and then replanted. This job is best done in the spring.

These adaptable onions will grow in any well drained soil, provided that it is reasonably fertile. The seeds can be sown outdoors after all the danger of frosts are over, directly into the cropping bed. Thin to 9" as soon as they are large enough to handle. Keep them well watered throughout the growing season. During the late autumn a mulch of well rotted compost or farm manure will be very beneficial.

Harvesting

Welsh onions can be harvested any time after early summer.

Preparing

The leaves do not dry well but can be frozen. Use a pair of scissors and snip them off into a plastic bag. They produce little rings which can then be frozen.

Cooking

Welsh Onions can make an excellent substitute for salad onions as they are earlier and indeed, hardier. Use them in salads, stir fry dishes or use them as you would chives.

Pak Choi

Pak Choi is a Chinese variety of white, celery mustard.

Growing

Pak Choi is grown in situ on the cropping area, which should be a well prepared rich, firm soil. The seeds are sown thinly directly into shallow drills, with the rows spaced at 15″ intervals. Sow the seeds during March/April and again in the late summer/early autumn. Thin the seedlings to 8″ apart as soon a they are large enough to handle. Pak Choi is a fairly long standing, slow to bolt plant.

Harvesting

Harvest when it is compact and well grown. Choose compact heads with round, smooth leaves and thick, pure white stalks.

Preparing

Separate the stems from each other and wash them well. Cut away the stalks from the leaves.

Cooking

Pak Choi is often used as one of the main ingredients in chow mein. The stalks can be used either raw or cooked inmuch the same way as celery. The smaller, more tender centre leaves are perfect for shredding raw for use in salads. The larger outer leaves are usually fried or lightly braised in the same way as lettuce.

Parsnips

This vegetable needs rich, well cultivated soil but not ground that has been freshly manured. Parsnips are one of the most resistant vegetables to frost. It is often said that a parsip never attains its true flavour until it has been well subjected to freezing weather.

Growing

Parsnips are grown from seed that are sown in groups of three in shallow drills with the rows 18″ apart. The groups of seed should be planted 5 to 6″ apart in the rows and are later singled out to 1 at each station.

Harvesting

Parsnips can be dug as required from October onwards and can be left in the ground all through the winter, although it is a good idea to lift a stock of roots to store in peat or sand in a cool place for use when the ground is frozen solid. Any roots left remaining in the ground in early spring must be lifted before they break into second growth or they will run straight off to seed.

Allow two medium sized roots for each serving. The roots should be smooth, firm and a good tapering shape.

Preparing

Wash, scrape or peel the roots. Remove the leaf crowns and any rootlets. They can be used whole, cut in halves, quarters, slices or diced.

Cooking

Cook covered in a little salted, boiling water until tender (approximately 30 minutes). Drain and season them with salt, pepper and melted butter. Serve hot and garnished with chopped parsley.

Mashed Parsnips
Mash 1½ lbs of cooked parsnips. Add 4fl oz of hot milk, 4 tablespoons of butter and salt and pepper to taste. Beat them all together until light and fluffy.

Roast Parsnips
Par-boil the roots, halved lengthwise until nearly tender. Drain, place into an ovenproof dish and baste them well with melted lard or dripping. Place them in a moderate oven (375°F Gas mark 5) until tender and golden brown.

Parsnips can also be roasted in the juices of a roasting meat joint.

Sautéed Parsnips.
Cut cooked parsnips into six pieces, lengthwise. Brown them lightly in melted butter and season to taste. Serve hot.

Glazed Parsnips
Par-boil 12 small to medium parsnips. Heat 2 tablespoons of butter or oil in a frying pan and add 2½oz of sugar and 2 tablespoons of water and stir well until the sugar has dissolved. Add the parsnips and cook them until well glazed and golden brown. Serve hot. (6 servings)

Parsnips can also be used diced in stews, soups and casseroles.

Peas | Garden

The green pea was originally a Near Eastern plant, but it is now grown extensively throughout the world. The pea can be used fresh, dried or frozen and can even be canned for use out of season. There are two main types of pea in general cutivation. They are usually classed as edible podded, which is dealt with in the next section and the shelling or green garden pea.

Growing

Peas require a fairly rich, well cultivated ground. Soil that has been prepared during the autumn and winter and allowed to settle can be advantageous, but this is not essential.

Drills for pea seed can be made in two ways. One way is to make a drill 2″ deep and 6″ wide and sow the seeds in two or three staggered rows within this trench. The distance between rows should be exactly corresponding to the height of the variety grown.

The dwarf growing varieties do not require any support, although they they do benefit from sticking.

The medium and tall growing peas will require support using either special nets or peasticks, which are usually hazel branches.

Peas can be sown in October, risking over wintering survival to, hopefully, obtain an early crop and can be quite successful, especially if some protection is available.

Generally peas are sown fortnightly from March to June to establish a regular succession of them.

Harvesting

Harvest them as soon as any pods are full, starting from

the bottom of the vines as these pods are the first to form. Regular picking helps the plants to give greater yields. Green peas should have fresh looking, bright green pods that feel velvety to the touch.

Preparing

Prepare and use peas as soon as possible after picking. Shell and wash them just prior to cooking. Allow 2lb of unshelled peas for four good servings.

Cooking

Cook peas covered, in 1″ of boiling, salted water for 8-10 minutes. Serve hot, seasoned with salt, pepper and butter.

Minted peas
Simply add sprigs of fresh mint to the cooking water.

Puréed Green Peas
Push the cooked peas through a sieve and beat them until light and fluffy with either hot milk or cream. Season to taste.

Creamed Peas
Fold the cooked peas into a medium white sauce. Serve hot, garnished with paprika.

Peas are an ingredient of macédoine, in which cooked peas are mixed in equal proportions with diced carrots and sweet corn kernels.

Peas | Mange Tout

Mange Tout (eat all), sugar peas and snow peas are just some of the names that this vegetable is known by.

Growing

Mange Tout are grown under the same conditions as the green pea. This plant grows to 4 – 5ft high so nets or sticks will be definitely needed. All other cultural details apply to mange tout as to green peas. The pods of this type of pea are picked before any seeds develop. A variety called 'Sugar Snap' has been developed which is a prolific cropper, with very succulent, edible pods.

Harvesting

Pick them regularly throughout the season to maintain the supply. Bright green and velvety pods which are almost translucent are the best. Embryo seeds can be just apparent but no development of them is acceptable.

Preparing

Wash, trim the ends and string the edges.

Cooking

Plunge into a little salted, boiling water. Cook until crisp and tender. Serve hot.

Any recipes for French beans can easily be adapted for mange tout.

Peppers | Chilli

If you can grow tomatoes successfully, you should be able to grow chillis. They are a little different in their needs but are just as easy to grow. They like a sunny patio, a big pot on a windowsill, or an unheated greenhouse.

Treat them as half-hardy annuals. The plants have a long growing season so they have to be grown indoors for protection against frost.

Growing

Seed is sown in late February to mid March. Sow either just a few seeds in several 3″ pots and pull out all except the strongest seedling, or scatter the seed thinly acrosss a larger pot and transplant the seedlings. Cover the seed to its own depth in compost and keep it at 20°C for the best germination.

Pot on the seedlings as they grow and if you are planning to keep the plants inside all summer, they will need at least a 30cm diameter pot when fully grown.

Harden off gradually from mid-May and plant out, if growing outdoors, by early June. They need a sheltered, well drained site in full sun. A very fertile soil is not vital.

Pinch out the growing tips occasionally to encourage them to bush out. Plants may need some support from twiggy branches pushed in around them, or they can be tied to a cane.

Harvesting

Pick peppers when they are green or coloured as you need them.

Peppers | Sweet

The sweet pepper is one of a number of peppers that are believed to have originated in South America. Other peppers thought to be of similar origin are the chilli, the pimento and the cayenne, all of which have the same cultural requirements as the sweet pepper. Sweet peppers are often called by their botanical name, *capsicum*.

Growing

Peppers are best grown as a protected crop, either in a greenhouse or a polytunnel. They should be planted into rich, well dug beds, allowing 3sq ft per plant. The plants are raised from seed sown 2 per 3″ pot, with the seedlings being thinned to one when large enough to handle. This sowing is made in late February or early March in a heated greenhouse or a month later in a coldframe. When the plants are 6 to 8″ high they are planted in the cropping beds.

Water them regularly and a light misting of water during flowering time, especially during the cool of the evening, will be beneficial in helping to set the fruit.

Harvesting

For green peppers, pick the fruit when they have reached a useable size.

For red peppers, allow the fruit to mature and ripen before picking.

Peppers should be well shaped, thick walled and firm to the touch, with an even, glossy colour.

Preparing

Peppers are used in several different ways. They can be eaten raw or cooked, diced, sliced or whole, depending on the recipe. To use whole, cut off the stem end of the peppers and scoop out the seeds and the white, pithy ribs. Very large fruits can be halved lengthways. Wash and drain them. Prepare as above and slice thickly for rings, or slice and dice.

Cooking

To use peppers raw in salads, slice or dice them finely and mix with other salad ingredients. As a garnish, use raw rings of pepper.

To use cooked, the peppers are usually diced and used as an ingredient in stews, casseroles and any other similar dishes.

Stuffed Peppers

Prepare the whole peppers as above. Par-boil them by dropping the shells into boiling water. Remove the pan from the heat and leave the peppers to stand in the water for 5 minutes. Drain them well, stuff with the selected filling and bakethem in a moderate oven (375°F Gas mark 5) until the peppers are tender and the tops are a golden brown.

The actual fillings can be any combination of cooked rice, fish, meats, cheeses, vegetables, eggs or pasta. Always top stuffed peppers with breadcrumbs or a mixture of grated cheeses and breadcrumbs.

Potatoes

Potatoes are originally natives of South America, having travelled to North America many years before the 16th century, when they were discovered and brought back to the UK.

Popular belief has given rise to the idea that potatoes are an exceptionally fattening food when, in actual fact, one medium sized potato has no more calories than a large apple. What is more, the potato gives such a wealth of food values to our diet that it is not surprising that it has become the main vegetable used in our daily menus.

One medium sized potato will actually provide about 10% of our daily requirements of vitamins B1, C and G as well as a high content of iron, phosphates and other minerals necessary for healthy life, with an energy factor of 120 calories.

Growing

Unless you have a really large garden with plenty of space I would not recommend growing main crop potatoes as they can be purchased reasonably cheaply and they use a lot of ground for a very long time that could be used for other valuable crops. I would, however, definitely recommend that you try to grow a few rows of early potatoes, just for the flavour alone.

Potatoes require a good, rich, well dug soil, preferably one that was heavily manured in the previous autumn. Just before planting the sets I recommend that you incorporate a good, general fertiliser at roughly 4oz per square yard.
Plant the sets, or seed (egg sized tubers from last season's crop) with a trowel 6″ deep and 15″ apart with 24″ between the rows. The seed can be 'chatted' before planting, by placing them in trays in a warm place for 6 to 8 weeks

before planting.

Tray the seeds up in January, so that they will be ready for planting in late March to early April. When the shoots appear, draw the earth up, over and around them. Continue earthing up as the growth increases until the potatoes are eventually growing on a ridge.

Harvesting

The tubers can be harvested as soon as they are big enough, in June or early July. Late main crop potatoes are harvested in October and stored for winter use by putting them in sacks or boxes in a dark, frost free place. An alternative storage method for potatoes and all other rootcrops is the system known as clamping. This method is suitable when there is a large crop to store. Details of how to build a clamp are are included below.

Good quality potatoes are generally clean, firm and free from growth cracks and other surface defects. The skin on new potatoes should always be thin and should rub off easily. The skin sets as the potatoes mature and will not rub off as easily, if at all, on older stock.

Any potato with green colouring on any of its surfaces should be avoided as they are usually bitter. This condition is known as 'sunburning.' In main crop potatoes, watch out for and discard any tubers that have a watery appearance, or have a black ring just under the skin when cut in half as these have been damaged by frost.

To build a clamp, mark out a circle or a large square, at least 3ft in diameter. Place a thick layer of straw within this area. Next, put a 6″ layer of the vegetable on the straw, followed by a further layer of straw. Continue in this manner, making each layer slightly smaller, until the clamp is 3 to 4ft high, finishing with a straw layer. Next, dig a trench around the bottom of the clamp using the soil to cover the clamp. This soil layer must be a minimum thickness of 3″ but preferably more. At the top of the clamp, leave some straw protruding from the soil. These act as vents to stop the clamp from over heating. In bad weather these vents must be covered. The roots within these clamps will keep well, provided the straw and the roots were kept as dry as possible whilst building the clamp and that the soil is packed tight when covering the clamp.

To use the vegetables, break into the clamp on the side away from the prevailing weather and remove sufficient vegetables for several days supply. Then completely seal the clamp back up again.

Preparing

The most food value is obtained from a potato when it is cooked in its 'jacket.' Therefore, whenever possible, cook potatoes in their skin, even if you intend to mash them. Boiled potatoes, done in their skin, retain a higher food factor than baked jacket potatoes.

Wash and scrub them with a brush if the potatoes are to be cooked in their skins. If not, peel them very thinly.

Cooking

There are literally dozens of ways to cook a potato, but many are just variations of a certain dish. I am including quite a few recipes here to try to show that the humble potato is not really quite so humble.

Boiled Potatoes.
Cook covered in boiling, salted water until tender. Drain, leave in the pan and keep on a very low heat until dry and fluffy.

Boiled variations
For new potatoes simply scrub or scrape. Do not peel.

Cheese Potato
Cover hot, cooked potatoes with a cheese sauce, then simply reheat and serve.

Parsley Potatoes
Add 2 tablespoons of melted butter and 3 tablespoons of chopped parsley. Shake well and serve.

Mashed Potatoes
Boil the potatoes until cooked. Mash them well. Season with salt and pepper. Add 2½fl oz of hot milk and 3 tablespoons of butter. Beat well until light and fluffy. Add a teaspoon of horseradish or even salad cream for a change.

Duchess Potatoes
Add 2 tablespoons of butter, salt and two lightly beaten

egg yolks to 1lb of hot, mashed potatoes. Blend together thoroughly. Shape into patties, croquettes or, using a forcing bag, make fancy mounds. (They can be frozen on open trays at his point). Put on a greased baking tray and brown in a hot oven. (450°F Gas mark 8). Serve at once.

Baked Potatoes (Jackets)
Scrub the potatoes, then dry and rub in seasoned, soft butter. Bake in a pre-heated hot oven (475°F Gas mark 8) until tender. When cooked, remove them from the oven, cut a cross on one side and squeeze until the cuts open. Dot the opening with butter and garnish with paprika before serving.

Stuffed, Baked Potatoes
Bake as above but halve the potatoes lengthways and scrape out the potato without damaging the shell. Mash the potato with meat, fish, vegetables or cheese and pile the mixture back into the shell, then garnish and serve.

Tatws Llaeth
Or new potatoes in buttermilk. Traditionally the first new potatoes to be lifted were used for this delicate and very nourishing dish. Scrape and cook the potatoes in salted, boiling water, preferably with a sprig of mint. When the potatoes are cooked drain them thoroughly, place each serving into a bowl and cover with butter milk. Eat at once.

Potato Anna
Peel and thinly slice 2lbs of potatoes. Layer the sliced

potato with grated onion and grated cheese mixed together. Repeat 3 times, then cover and bake in a hot oven (450°F Gas mark 7) for 30 minutes and uncover and cook for a further 5 minutes. Serve hot, inverted on a platter. This dish is similiar to a Lancashire dish called Pan-Heggerty. (Serves 6)

Scalloped Potatoes
Peel 2lbs of potatoes and slice thinly. Layer them in a greased casserole dish and make up a medium thick white sauce. Mix in 2 tablespoons of chopped onions and pour over the potatoes. Cover and bake in a moderate oven (350°F Gas mark 4) for an hour. Uncover and bake until golden brown. (Serves 4)

Roast Potatoes
Peel the potatoes. Cut them in half or quarters according to size. Place in a baking tin with ¼″ of melted lard or oil. Cook in a moderate oven (375°F Gas mark 5), turning and basting occasionally for one and a half hours, or until nicely brown and crisp all over. The roasting time can be shortened by par-boiling the potatoes for 15 minutes before roasting. If par-boiled, remove them from the water, drain and 'fluff up' the sides by shaking them lightly against the sides of the pan. Roast potatoes can also be cooked in the juices of the meat.

Potato Chips/French Fries
Wash, peel and cut the potatoes lengthways into strips and soak in cold water for an hour. Drain and dry them well. Heat a pan of deep fat to 375° F (until smoking).

Fry the chips, a few at a time, until lightly brown, then drain. (They can be open frozen at this point). Just before serving, return to the hot fat and fry until crisp and golden brown. Drain, season with salt and serve immediately.

Game chips
Cut peeled potatoes into very thin slices and fry as above.

Lyonnaise Potatoes
Boil the potatoes in their jackets, then remove the skin and slice them ¼" thick. Mix thinly with sliced onions in equal proportions. Season with salt and pepper. Finally, fry them in hot fat until brown and crispy.

Potato and Celery Soup
Melt 2oz of butter and gently fry 1lb of peeled and diced potatoes, 2 diced onions and 5 stalks of chopped celery for 5 minutes.

Add 1½ pints of stock and salt and pepper. Bring to the boil, cover the pan and allow it to simmer for about 40 minutes, then sieve or liquidize. Add ¼ pint of milk. Reheat and grate in a little nutmeg. Serve at once.

Radish

There are two types of radish grown, one is the summer radish and the other is a winter radish. The winter radish grows a lot bigger than the summer one and is slightly hotter in flavour. The winter radish is lifted and stored for use during the winter months.

Growing

Radishes are grown in fairly rich ground as they need to be very quick growing or else they become coarse and woody. Because they are quick growing they are ideal for catch-cropping on celery ridges and between rows of longer growing crops. The seeds are sown in drills ½″ deep and 6″ apart.

Sow every 10 days from March to September using the summer variety.

The winter radish can be sown in July or September, but never earlier than July.

Harvesting

Summer radishes are pulled from the rows as required for use, but the larger, winter varieties have to be thinned to 6″ apart to allow them to develop. Winter varieties are lifted and stored in dry sand in a frost free place and used as required during the winter.

Radishes should be of a good shape, smooth and crisp.

Preparing

Wash and remove the roots. Only damaged leaves should be removed from the summer crops, leaving the good ones intact. Summer Radishes are used whole, or sliced thinly. The winter varieties are always served sliced.

Cooking

Although it is not usual to cook radishes, they can be boiled in salted water in a covered pot for 8 minutes. Serve them very hot with butter.

To serve raw

Use them cold and crisp with dips as an hors d'oeuvres. Slice them thinly, or grate them for use in vegetable and green salads.

Salsify and Scorzonera

Two less commonly known and used vegetables are salsify and scorzonera. They are often mistaken for each other, but it is easy to recognize either one from the other by the root colour. Scorzonera roots are black, but salsify has light brown roots.

An oyster like flavour is common to both, as are the requirements for cultivation, the culinary details and operation. Both vegetables are grown for their roots which are of a delicate flavour.

Growing

Both vegetables are grown in situ and require a long growing season. Sow the seeds thinly in shallow drills in rows 12 to 15″ apart. Thin the seedlings to 6″ when big enough to handle. Hoe them regularly to control the weeds and water well in dry weather.

Harvesting

Lift the roots in late autumn after the first frosts, as this improves the flavour. Remove the tops and store in dry sand for use as required during the winter. Smooth, firm and straight but tapering roots that are about the size of a medium parsnip are ideal.

Preparing

Scald the roots by dipping them in boiling water, then scrape and cut them into small pieces. Place the cut pieces into cold water with several lemon slices or 2 teaspoons of vinegar to prevent discolouration. Drain them well.

Cooking

Cover with unsalted, boiling water and cover and cook until tender – about 30 minutes. Drain and serve them hot, seasoned with salt, pepper and butter.

Sautéed Salsify

Cook the salsify as above, then drain well and roll it in seasoned flour or breadcrumbs. Sauté in hot oil until nicely brown all over.

Creamed Salsify

Fold the cooked salsify into a medium thick white sauce. Reheat it and serve hot, garnished with chopped parsley.

Salsify Eggs.

Cook 3 roots of salsify in boiling water. Drain and dice them into small pieces. Melt 1oz of butter in a frying pan. Add the salsify, seasoning it well with salt and pepper. Add 1 teaspoon of lemon juice and keep over a moderate heat for 5 minutes. Beat four eggs and add 2 tablespoons of single cream. Pour this into the pan with the salsify and gently cook until it is just set and creamy, stirring all the time. Turn on to a warm serving dish and surround with hot, fried croutons.

Spinach

Spinach is another old vegetable that has been grown for many hundreds of years, having first been introduced into Europe by the Moors.

Spinach has a very high food rating, being rich in vitamins A and C, as well as worthwhile amounts of iron, riboflavin and some calcium.

There are two types of spinach in general cultivation; the round-seeded summer spinach and the prickly seeded winter spinach. They are both grown entirely for their leaves which are picked off the plants as soon as they are a useable size.

Growing

Spinach is best grown in soil that leans towards heaviness rather than light, sandy soils as dry light soils tend to make the spinach run prematurely to seed, especially in hot weather. Sow in well prepared and manured soil in 1″ deep drills with rows 12″ apart. Thin the plants to 6″ apart in the rows as soon as they are big enough.

Round seeded spinach needs to be sown every two weeks from mid March until mid July, with a sowing in mid August of the winter prickly seeded type. Keep it well watered in dry weather. Two good varieties are 'long standing summer' and 'long standing winter.'

Harvesting

Allow 2lbs of fresh spinach for four portions. Use well developed, crisp, green young leaves.

Preparing

Wash it at least twice using salty water for the first wash.

Remove any coarse main ribs from the leaves.

Cooking

Cook covered, using only the water that clings to the leaves after the initial soak. Boil for a few minutes. Drain and chop, then serve at once, hot, seasoned with salt, pepper and a little vinegar or lemon juice. Butter can be used instead of vinegar.

Creamed Spinach

Cook the spinach as above and keep it hot. Melt 2 tablespoons of butter and blend in 1½ tablespoons of flour with a dash of nutmeg. Stir in ¼ pint of milk and ¼ pint of chicken stock (or half a pint of milk and a chicken stock cube) with a little grated onion. Cook, stirring continuously until it thickens. Add the hot, drained spinach, fold in and serve.

Spinach Timbales

Combine 1½ lbs of chopped, cooked spinach with 3 lightly beaten eggs, 2fl oz of cream, 2 tablespoons of melted butter and 2½oz of soft, fine breadcrumbs. Season with half a teaspoon of salt and mix well.

Take six greased ramekin dishes and fill them three quarters full. Place them in a little water in a shallow baking tray and bake in a moderate oven (350°F Gas mark 4) until firm (about 35 minutes). Take them out of the moulds and serve with a white sauce and garnished with a slice of hard boiled egg.

Squashes

Squashes are all of American Indian origin and the name refers to any plant that is a member of the *'cucubitae'* family. Although the cucumber is a member of this group, it is not usually classed as a squash. The most common squashes grown in the UK are marrows, courgettes (which are small, undeveloped marrows), pumpkins and melons. These are known as summer squashes. There are others, known as winter squashes, which require a more temperate climate than our own.

Growing

All the above squashes are grown outdoors, except for the melon which requires the protection of a greenhouse or a coldframe. All prefer an open soil with plenty of well rotted compost or manure worked into it. They will achieve good results when planted on well decomposed compost heaps. Sow the seeds, 2 to a 3″ pot, in late April/early May. Single out the plants, selecting the strongest and plant out on the cropping sites in June, when the risk of frost is over.

Note that all these plants carry separate male and female flowers and will often need cross pollinating by hand to increase the crop.

Pinch out the growing tips after 3 leaves on trailing varieties to encourage the growth of laterals. When cross pollinating by hand, pick off the male flowers, preferably around mid-day when the pollen is flowing well, and insert the stamens into the female flower, ensuring that the stamens and female pistils come into contact with each other. The female flower will have an embryo fruit behind the shoulders of the flower.

Bush varieties will not require any stopping or thinning.

Squashes | Courgettes

Courgettes are ready for cutting when they are 4 to 5″ long. There is a bush variety called 'courgette' that has been specially bred to produce prolific crops.

Harvesting

Use fresh, young squashes and courgettes with a smooth and tender skin.

Preparing

Wash them but do not peel. Cut off the stem and blossom ends and slice them into ¼″ slices.

Cooking

Cook them covered, with very little boiling, salted water until they are tender after approximately 10 minutes. Drain and serve hot, seasoned with salt, pepper and butter.

Baked Courgettes

Cut the cleaned courgettes in half, lengthways. Place the cut side downwards in a greased oven dish. Dot with butter and chopped bacon and season with salt and pepper and bake until tender in a moderate over (375°F Gas mark 5) for about 30 minutes. Serve with hollandaise sauce.

Stuffed Courgettes

Clean 6 medium sized courgettes and remove the ends. Cook whole for 5 minutes in boiling, salted water, then cut the courgettes in half, lengthways. Scoop out the flesh from the shells.

Chop the flesh into small pieces and mix it with 12oz of fresh, cooked or canned, sweetcorn kernels, 2 beaten eggs and 1oz of finely chopped or grated onion. Season well.

Heap the mixture into the courgette shells and place them in an ovenproof dish. Cover with grated cheese and bake in a moderate oven (350°F Gas mark 4) for 30 minutes or until golden brown.

Italian Style Courgettes

Sauté a sliced onion in butter or oil until transparent yellow. Add 1lb of sliced courgettes. Cook, stirring occasionally, for 5 minutes, then add 8oz of canned, or fresh tomatoes. If fresh, remove the skin beforehand by piecing with a knife in several places and pouring boiling water over them. Once cooled, the skin will peel away with little effort. Season, cover and cook until tender on a low heat for approximately 30 minutes. Serve hot.

Squashes | Vegetable Marrows

Marrows should be cut while still young and tender when they are about 12″ in length. A test for the tenderness of marrows can be made by pushing a thumb nail into one of the marrow ribs at the stalk end. Even a stored marrow should still have skin that can be pierced with a thumb nail.

Allow 2lb for 4 servings and use smooth, tender skinned fruits.

Preparing

Wash the marrow well and cut it into rings, blocks, dice it or leave it whole, according to the recipe. Remove the seeds.

Cooking

Use the basic courgette recipe, cutting the marrow into 12 pieces. Season and serve hot.

Poor Man's Goose (Meat Stuffed Marrow)

Clean and remove the ends of a large marrow. Leave it whole, but remove all the seeds. Mix 4oz of sausage meat with 4oz of cooked, long-grained rice and season with salt, pepper and mixed herbs. Stuff the marrow shell with this mixture and place it in an ovenproof dish with a little water. Cover and bake it in a slow oven (275°F Gas mark

3) for 2½ hours, or until tender. Serve hot, cut into rings and with a rich gravy.

Marrow Provencale

Cook 2oz of chopped onion with 1 chopped garlic clove in 2fl oz of oil for 3 minutes without colouring. Add 1lb of marrow, cut into 1″ cubes and season with salt and pepper. Chop 1lb of tomatoes and add them to the mix. Cover and simmer gently for an hour until tender.

Marrow and Onion Savoury

Peel, de-seed and cut a marrow into 1″ cubes. Layer the marrow and 1lb of thinly sliced onion in a greased pie dish. End with a layer of marrow uppermost. Dot with butter. Cover it with foil and cook in a preheated oven at 350°F Gas mark 4 for about 1½ hours, or until the marrow is cooked. This dish will cook on the lower shelf under a roast and will make for the perfect accompaniment.

In fact, any of the recipes prescribed for courgettes can also be used for marrow.

Squashes | Pumpkin

Pumpkins are allowed to ripen and mature on the bines, not being cut until the bines actually die. Very often pumpkins, especially those required for show purposes, are given extra feeding with sugar water, using a wick running from a bottle containing the sugar water into the stem where the fruit joins it.

Many specialist growers who do show pumpkins will only allow 1 fruit to develop on each plant.

Preparing

Wash well, peel, remove the seeds and dice the flesh.

Cooking

Cook covered in a little boiling water for 15 minutes or until tender.

Pumpkin Cake

Sift together 3oz of plain flour, 3 teaspoons of baking powder, half a teaspoon of salt, a ¼ teaspoon of bicarbonate of soda, 1½ teaspoons of cinnamon, half a teaspoon of ground ginger and half a teaspoon of mixed spice.

Cream 6oz of butter, gradually add 6oz of brown with 4oz of caster sugar and cream well. Add a whole egg and beat it well. Add 2 further egg yolks, one at a time, beating until fluffy. Gradually add the flour mix alternately with 6fl oz of milk, beating continuously until the mixture is smooth. Stir in 6oz of grated pumpkin.

Line two 8″ sandwich tins. Fill with the mixture and bake for 35 minutes, or until done, in a moderate oven (350°F Gas mark 5). Cool and decorate with fluffy orange icing.

Pumpkin Pie

Line an 8″ pie dish with uncooked pastry. Using a large mixing bowl, mix together 3oz of brown sugar, 2 teaspoons of flour, a ¼ teaspoon of salt and 1½ teaspoons of mixed spice. Add 8oz of cooked pumpkin, a ½ pint of evaporated milk, 1 beaten egg and 2 tablespoons of black treacle.

Blend them well until smooth. Pour the mixture into the prepared pie dish and bake in the centre of a moderate oven (375°F Gas mark 5) for 45 minutes, until firm. Serve hot with custard or cold with thick cream.

Pumpkin can also be used to make soups or used as a vegetable.

Squashes | Melon

Melons can be grown practically all year round, provided that a heated greenhouse capable of maintaining a temperature of 65-70°F (18-20°C) is available. If this facility is available, sow the seeds singly in 3″ pots from January to late May.

The plants are planted on ridges of rich soil, either on the floor in a greenhouse with glass down to the ground, or on benches in the low walled type of greenhouse. The beds need to be 2ft wide and at least 6″ deep.

The ideal compost for these beds would consist of fibrous loam with a leaf mould and some well rotted manure added. Set the plants 2ft apart and train as single stems to wires stretched tightly from one end to the other. Pinch out the growing tip when the plants reach about 30-36″

and allow 4 side shoots to develop.

Female flowers will develop on these side shoots and these must be fertilized with pollen from the male flowers. This has to be done by hand, either as described above (see Squashes/Growing p.121) or by transferring the pollen with a camel hair brush. Allow 4 fruits to develop per plant. As soon as the fruits start swelling, stop all other lateral growths. Water them freely until the melons start emitting their characteristic smell when they are nearly ripe. Feed them occasionally with a liquid fertilizer during the growing season. The melons may need supporting with nets as they grow.

Frame grown melons are sown in pots during April, ready for planting out into frames in June. A 4ft x 4ft frame will accommodate 2 plants. Stop the plants after the fourth leaf and, again, allow 4 side shoots to grow for developing fruit. Further cultivation of frame melons is the same as for greenhouse fruit.

Harvesting

Melons should be firm when ripe. They are ready to harvest when they yield slightly to finger pressure near the stalk end. A ripe melon will also emit a fragrant odour that is very apparent.

Wash them well and trim the ends finely, but do not peel.

Cooking

Melons are not usually cooked but I have included a delicious hot melon dish.

Melon Ball Cocktails
Cut balls from the melon flesh using a melon ball cutter or a small teaspoon. Chill them and place in a sundae glass. Sweeten with a syrup made by dissolving 4oz of sugar in 5fl oz of hot water. Cook this for 5 minutes then add 2 tablespoons of lemon juice, 2 tablespoons of lime juice and 2 tablespoons of orange juice. Cool and pour over the chilled melon balls.

Chilled Melon
Cut the melon into 8 wedges. Remove the seeds, chill it and serve on crushed ice on a bed of lettuce with caster sugar and ground ginger. Melon slices can also be served with soft fruits piled into the hollows.

Laced Melon
Cut out a plug at the top of a melon. Remove the seeds. Pour 8fl oz of port or sherry into the hollow. Replace the plug and chill in the fridge for 6 to 8 hours. Serve using the juices as a dressing. Rum or any other spirits can be used as an alternative to fortified wines.

Baked Melon
Cut two small melons in half. Remove the seeds. Mix together 1½lb of sliced peaches, 4oz of sugar and a ¼ teaspoon of ground mace. Fill the melons with the peach

mixture, making a decorative pattern with the top layer of slices. Bake in a hot oven (425°F Gas mark 7) for 15 minutes. Serve at once, garnished with mint sprigs.

Swedes and Turnips

The Swede is a yellow fleshed turnip, but the flavour is less pungent than the white turnip. The swede has been a rather neglected vegetable in the past, mainly because it was seen as a winter fodder for cattle. Swedes have a high Vitamin B1 content and make an excellent vegetable if properly cooked. The best commercial crops of Swede are said to be grown on the red soil of Devon, but they will give a reasonable crop on any well cultivated land.

Growing

Swedes are one of the easiest crops to grow as they tend to look very much after themselves. Sow the seeds thinly during May or June in shallow drills 15" apart. Thin the seedlings to 8 in the rows.

Harvesting

You should harvest when ready in the autumn. Roots about the diameter of an average saucer are ideal. Swedes can be stored in clamps (See p.109) for winter use.

Swedes should have a smooth skin, be firm and feel heavy

for their size.

Preparing

Scrub the swede clean. Peel it thinly just before cooking. They can be used whole, sliced or diced.

Cooking

Cook covered in a little salted water. Whole roots will require 25 to 30 minutes cooking time with diced or sliced ones needing just half this time. Serve hot, seasoned with salt, pepper and butter. Swedes can be mashed with a little hot milk, butter and seasoning.

Creamed Swedes
Reheat some cooked, diced swede with a little double cream and serve hot.

Glazed Swede
Cook ¾lb of diced swede until tender. Drain well. Melt 3 tablespoons of butter and 3 tablespoons of golden syrup in a frying pan a touch of ground mace. Add the swede and cook slowly, turning continuously until lightly browned.

Casseroled Swede
Place some diced, raw swede into an ovenproof casserole dish. Season with salt and pepper and dot with butter. Add consommé to cover the bottom of the dish. Bake in a moderate oven (350°F Gas mark 4) until soft for approximately 45 minutes.

Swiss and Rhubarb Chard

Swiss and rhubarb chard are similar vegetables, the main difference being that rhubarb chard has long crimson stems and dark foliage while swiss chard has white stalks and lighter green leaves. Neither of the chards produce edible roots.

Growing

Sow the seeds in April through to July in shallow drills 28″ apart on the cropping. Thin the seedlings to 6″ apart as soon as possible.

Harvesting

Harvest by pulling off the leaves in a similar way to spinach. Use large, clean, tender leaves and stems.

Preparing

Wash it well, cut out the thick mid ribs and cut them into small pieces. Shred the leaves.

Cooking

Cook the leafy portion like spinach. The stalks are cooked for a few minutes in salted, boiling water and served separately from the leaves which should be still crisp. Melted butter or hollandaisse sauce are good accompaniments for this vegetable.

Tomato

Tomatoes are not really vegetables. They are a fruit. When tomatoes were first introduced to this country from the Americas, the fruits were very small compared to the modern varieties and were called 'love apples' as it was believe that they had aphrodisiac qualities. It was also believed, in some circles, that they were a deadly poison. It would seem very unlikely that anyone in today's environment might have any such beliefs, especially as it is now a well known fact that tomatoes are one of the richest sources of both vitamin A and C, as well as being a delicious red fruit to eat.

Growing

Tomatoes can be grown both indoors, under glass, or outside in warm, sunny, sheltered sites. There are a great many different varieties in both single stem and bush types. The advantages of growing the bush varieties outside are that they need no staking or side shooting, while still producing good crops. One good variety of this type is the 'Amateur.' Well known indoor varieties include 'Money Maker,' which is a prolific cropper and 'Ailsa Craig.' There are also many new F1 hybrid varieties available.

Glasshouse Cultivation

Sow the seeds in boxes of good seed compost during January, February or March, in a very warm greenhouse with a minimum temperature of 60-65°F (16°C). Prick out the seedlings into 3″ pots when large enough to handle, making sure to touch only the cotyledon leaves, which are the first leaves to appear. When the plants are 6″ high they are ready to plant into their growing sites.

This can be done in a variety of ways:

They can be planted into 9″ pots containing good compost or into 9″ bottomless pots for planting on in grow bags. The method that I prefer is to plant directly into prepared beds in the greenhouse, with the plants 18″ apart and rows 3ft apart. Each plant is tied to a cane or supported by a soft string suspended from the rafters.

Each plant is trained as a single stem by pinching out all the side shoots as soon as they appear. Stop the plants when they reach the roof glass. Water them sparingly at first, then more freely when the fruit trusses start to appear. Feed weekly when the first fruits are set. Tap the stem gently around midday and gently spray them with water to assist pollination and fruit set.

When the bottom trusses have set fruit which has started to ripen, remove the bottom leaves from the main stem to allow more light to the fruit. Pick fruits regularly as soon as they ripen. A minimum temperature of 55°F must be maintained for growing tomatoes.

Outdoor Cultivation

Sow the seeds in late March/early April in the greenhouse. Treat the seedlings as before. Move them to coldframes in early May to harden them off. They will be ready to plant out in June. Plant them 18″ apart with rows 30″ between them. Do train the plants as before but stop the main stem after 4 trusses have set. Give plenty of water in dry weather and pick the fruit as it ripens.

Harvesting

Tomatoes should be firm, well-shaped and not over ripe. Most importantly, they should smell like tomatoes! Once bitten you will never go back to the tasteless, too perfectly formed tomatoes found stacked high in supermarkets. (It makes me smile at the marketing guru who came up with the 'flavour-grown tomatoes' gem they now blazen on their expensive range. Are they admitting, then, that all the others have no flavour?)

Preparing

Wash them well. There is no need to peel tomatoes as the skins are edible. If a recipe calls for peeled tomatoes, the easiest way to peel them is to gently pierce the skin in several places with a sharp knife. Then leave them in boiling water for a few minutes. Once removed and cooled, the skins can be removed without a problem.

Cooking

Quarter some peeled tomatoes, place them in a pan and simmer, covered but without water, for about 10 minutes. Season them with salt, pepper and chopped onion.

For salads they can be sliced thinly or thickly, halved, quartered or chopped.

Tomato Provencale

Stone and chop 2oz of black olives. Wash 8 medium, firm tomatoes and thinly cut 1 slice from the bottom of each one. Using cocktail sticks, skewer a whole olive to these slices. Scoop out the pulp of the tomatoes and allow the shells to thoroughly drain.

Heat 3 tablespoons of oil in a frying pan. Add 2oz of chopped onion with 2 cloves of garlic. Cook until soft and golden. Add ¾lb of sausage meat and cook slowly for 15 minutes or until nicely browned. Drain off the oil and the fat. Season with salt, pepper and chopped parsley. Add the chopped olives and mix well before stuffing the mixture into the tomato shells. Cook in a moderate oven (375°F Gas mark 5) for 15 minutes. Top with the tomato slices and cook for a further 5 minutes.

Tomatoes can be stuffed and baked using this method, but with any combination of cooked meats, vegetable and/or rice, or topped with fried breadcrumbs intead of tomato.

Marinated Tomatoes

Take 6 medium tomatoes. Wash and cut them into slices or chunks. Put them into a salad bowl and add 1 chopped garlic clove, 1 tablespoon of grated onion, 1 teaspoon of mixed herbs and 1 teaspoon of chopped parsley. Pour over 4 table spoons of French dressing, toss lightly, cover and refrigerate for several hours.

Tomato Soup

Sweat 1 large onion in oil until it is soft. Add 3lb of finely diced ripe, peeled tomatoes, some tomato purée, a crushed clove of garlic, some seasoning and chopped basil leaves (optional). Keep stiring over a low heat.

Pour 1 pint of chicken or vegetable stock over it and let it simmer for 30 - 40 minutes. Grate a potato into the soup; this thickens it up nicely. Then let it simmer for another 10 - 15 minutes.

Finally, blend until smooth and serve on a cold day with bread and butter.

Dorothy Soup

Finely chop 2lbs of onions and lighly fry them until soft, but not brown. Slice 1lb of tomatoes and add to the pan. Continue cooking and stiring, until the onions and tomatoes are soft. Pour on ¾ pint of water and bring to the boil. Pour the water, toms and onions through a sieve.

Put this vegetable purée to one side, keeping the tomato flavoured stock, which you can freeze and use another time.

In the pan put one large tablespoon of oatmeal with another ¾ pint of water and bring this to the boil for 10 minutes. Add the vegetable purée to the oatmeal, season with salt, pepper and one level teaspoon of sugar. Simmer for 20 minutes, adding more water if the soup becomes too thick. Taste and season again if necessary. Serve with a little chopped parsley as a garnish.
You can add a tablespoon of cream prior to serving.

Cold Stuffed Tomatoes
Hard boil 2 eggs and put them to one side to cool down. Meanwhile pick 4 to 6 firm tomatoes, stand them stalks down and cut a thin slice from the round end which is now uppermost. Save these slices which you will need later. Remove the pulp, sprinkly lightly with salt and turn them upside down and allow to drain.

Drain a can of sardines in oil, remove the tails and backbone and mash them. Mix the eggs into 2oz of softened butter and add 1 teaspoon of mustard and 1 teaspoon of chopped parsley. Mix in the mashed sardines and fill the tomato shells with the mixture. Put the lids back on and serve cold.

Herbs

There are several different ways to grow herbs. Most are hardy in our summers and can be grown outdoors. This is certainly ideal for many of the annual herbs. Then there are the perennials that are also sown outdoors but which are then transferred to their final positions, or even left in the seedbed, thinned out and allowed to mature. Finally there are the biennials that are ready the following year. These are also sown outside.

Professional growers, and now also a growing band of enthusiastic amateurs, are successfully using polytunnels or greenhouses to considerably extend their crops.

Growing herbs outdoors

I find that raised beds, about a foot high and made by laying old railway sleepers on their sides, 1 wide, but any number long, are ideal for growing herbs. I find that once the beds are built it is best to fill up the centres with spent mushroom compost, but which still has plenty of life left in it. Making these beds like this gives an almost sterile organic growing area for the production of herbs. Raised beds also have the advantage of being easily covered by fleecy sheets to ward off any frost, pests etc. but one disadvantage is that they do need watering quite often, although a drip feeding/watering system will take care of this chore.

Now we have our bed(s) in place and settled in nicely, we can start to think about sowing the various seeds. I personally like to divide my beds up, about one sleeper in length and broadcast the seed very lightly over the surface of the bed. I then take a wire rake and lightly rake in the seed, water it gently and cover it with fleece if needed.

Alternatively, the bed can be drilled out in ½" drills and the seed sown very thinly in these rows, then covered with compost, watered and covered with the fleece.

Whichever way you choose to do it, thin them to 1 every 3 to 6" as soon as the plants are big enough and then let them grow on to either harvesting for drying, for fresh use or for marketing.

Growing herbs undercover

There are 2 ways to grow under plastic. The first is to use ordinary seedtrays and the other is to use the cheap, modular pots that are now on the market. The method of growing herbs in ordinary seedtrays is exactly the same as growing any other plant by this method.

You sow the seed thinly in trays in a ground bark type of compost and then water them well. Put them on the staging with a little, or no heat, depending on the type of herb and the outside temperature. Cover them with either glass or plastic. Most of the seeds will sprout after 10 days. As soon as the plants begin to appear, remove the glass. Do watch out for them drying out during this delicate stage.

As soon as the plants are large enough to handle they must be pricked out, either as a clump in a 3½″ pot, or singularly in the same sized pot to produce specimen plants.

The other method is usually used for the big, shrub like plants such as rosemary, rue, sage etc. This method is far easier as it reduces the amount of time used for the pricking out of the plants. Sow a dozen or so seeds in each section of a modular try. I usually use either 25 or 40 hole modules. Cover them lightly with vermiculite or perlite or even compost and water them well in. I prefer to use vermiculite as I get a very even germination but perlite certainly makes a first class top dressing for the finished product, especially when the plants are out on racks to sell.

As they grow these plants should not need any thinning out, and you will find that the 25 modules can be broken up into single pots and then slid into a paper sleeve when they are ready for sale.

Angelica

Sometimes called garden angelica or root of the devil, it is a native of Europe, Asia and North America, but it is widely grown as a garden plant throughout the whole world. It is a biennial or short lived perennial plant and produces flowers in its second year. The flowers are sweetly scented with greenish white heads and they appear from late spring/early summer.

Growing

Angelica can only be grown from seed, but as the seed loses its viability virtually overnight, it is by far the best way to sow the seed during the autumn. If this is really not possible, store it in a refrigerator and sow in the spring in tiny pinches. As the plants to not like to be moved, sow the seed where the crop is to grow and thin out all the weedy type plants when they are big enough to handle. The plant can be difficult to accomodate in small areas. You will find that it dies right back over winter.

Make sure that the soil is deep and moist, with well rotted compost to help retain the moisture. Angelica needs plenty of water to produce well, but if in summer the leaves start to turn a yellowish brown it is a sign that it needs water fast.

Harvesting

Leaves for fresh use are available from spring onwards. For drying, pick from early summer until they start to flower. Roots can be harvested and dried in the second year, immediately after flowering.

Using

The young leaves of wild angelica are used as an aromatic salad leaf, while the seeds are often used in pastries by confectioners. It is well known as a decoration for cakes and you can purchase a bright emerald, plastic version but this cannot be compared with the homemade pale, green, candied angelica.

Recipe for Candied Angelica

Select young tender stems and cut them into 4″ pieces. Put them into a saucepan with just enough water to cover the stems and simmer until tender. Strain and remove the outside skin. Then replace in the pan with a little water to cover the stems and bring to the boil. Strain at once and let the stems cool.

When cool, weigh them and add equal amounts of granulated sugar in a covered dish. Leave them in a cool place for 2 days then return them to the saucepan, including all the syrup. Bring it all slowly to the boil and simmer, stirring often, until the angelica has a good colour. Strain it once again, this time discarding all the liquid (or, better still, pour it over melon or fruit salad) and sprinkle with caster sugar, using as much sugar as will stick to the angelica.

Put it into a warm oven (200°F Gas mark ¼) to completely dry it out. Store it in an airtight container, using sheets of greaseproof paper between layers.

Crushed Anglica leaves will improve the air in a car and decrease the chances of travel sickness and using the young leaves in tea drunk last thing at night relieves tension, nervous headaches, anaemia, coughs and colds.
The tea must not, however, be given to anybody suffering from diabetes and large doses must be avoided, as they

first stimulate, but can then paralyse the nervous system.

Basil | Sweet

Originating from India where it is considered sacred to the Gods, basil now grows wild in Mediterranean areas. It is a most useful herb and a key ingredient for many Italian and Indian dishes and is great when used fresh in salads. The freshly picked taste is far superior to the dried variety.

There are a number of other varieties of Basil worth seeking out from specialist nurseries: cinnamon basil (*ocimum basilcum*), lemon basil (*ocimum citriodorum*), purple basil (*ocimum basilcum purpurea*), red rubin basil (*ocimum basilcum*) - similar to sweet basil but with very darkly coloured leaves - and Thai basil (*ocimum sp.*) which is very spicy and is used in Indian cooking.

Growing

Sow very thinly in 3″ pots in March/April. Cover it lightly with compost, water well and then place in sealed polythene bags or cover with glass. Water from beneath. Keep the compost moist but not overly wet.

After germination, remove the pots from the bags or glass and place them in a light position, but away from direct sunlight. Thin them to 3 plants per pot when the plants are approximately 2″ tall.

To grow them on in pots, harden off the plants which have been raised indoors and then move them outdoors once all danger of frost has passed. When the plants are established with a good root system, divide them into separate plants and pot each of them into 6″ pots. Pinch out any growing tips regularly to produce bushy plants.

To grow on in situ do as above, but plant the divided plants in beds or borders 12″ apart.

Harvesting

The leaves can be picked about 6 weeks after planting. If harvesting for drying, cut the leaves just before the flowers open.

Using

Basil always seems well partnered by tomatoes, pasta and salads. Use it sparingly as it has quite a strong taste.

Although fresh basil has a far better flavour than its dried counterpart, you can dry the plant by tying the stems together and hanging them upside down in a dry, warm and dark place until dry. Then simply crush/crumble the leaves into pieces and store in a jar. Basil will retain almost all its flavour if placed in small plastic bags and kept in the freezer.

You can make an oil infused with basil by adopting a traditional method of preserving herbs. Layer the leaves in a jar or other suitable container and lightly salt them. An old olive oil bottle would be ideal. Cover them with a layer of olive oil, seal tightly and then put them in the fridge. You can then take out the leaves as you need them. The oil will become infused with the basil essence, making it ideal for use in dressings or in pasta dishes.

Bay | Sweet

It was worn by the Greeks as a garland round their heads. They named it laurel but it is also known as sweet bay and is one of the most versatile herbs. The bay laurel can be grown as a tall evergreen tree with its glossy foliage or in containers, which is more the norm in the UK.

The leaves are a major part of a 'bouquet garni' and it is often used to flavour stews and meat dishes, but the leaves themselves are quite indigestible and they must be removed before eating.

Growing

I do not recommend sowing this from seed as success is erratic at best, and the seeds can take as long as 3 months to even sprout a shoot. The main problem is that the seeds may begin to rot before they can germinate and even cuttings can take a long time to take. The best option is to grow a pot grown specimen and place it outdoors in a sunny, sheltered place. Re-pot it into larger pots as necessary.

The Bay, especially when young, does not like frost. If frost does cause all the leaves to turn brown, cut the plant back to 6″ above the soil level. In spring new shoots should begin to appear from the base of the plant.

Harvesting

Pick individual young leaves from all over the plant, picking them early in the day and drying them out quickly, away from direct sunlight. Put them under a weight and between kitchen paper for an hour or so, in order to prevent them from curling. When stored in an airtight container they will keep for up to a year.

Using

They go particularly well with meat dishes, especially stews, casseroles and meat pasta sauces and are used in Bouquet Garni.

Bouquet Garni

Get some cheesecloth, which is commonly used for straining. You can still buy this from a haberdashers. Cut it into 6″ squares and in each square place bay leaves, parsley and thyme. Tie up the squares with string to form little bundles of herbs. Tie the string to leave a loop that can be strung over a handle when cooking, to make removal from the pan or casserole dish easier.

Borage

Star shaped, blue flowers make borage a particularly attractive herb, and the leaves taste a little like cucumber, making it popular in salads. It loves rich soil and full sun, but can tolerate poorer soil and slight shade. It is an excellent companion plant for tomatoes, squashes and strawberries and, if planted near a tomato plant, it is said to improve the flavour of the fruit.

Growing

Seeds can be sown throughout the season, and once growth is established it will continue to seed itself. Place plants close together so that they can support each other. Sow outdoors in small pots or seed trays or, alternatively, plant directly into the ground in a dry sunny position. Sow the seeds thinly and lightly cover with compost.

Once the seeds have germinated and the plants are 2″ high, thin them out to 3 plants per pot. When the plants are established and have healthy roots you can then divide them into 6″ pots or 12″ apart, if planted directly into the ground.

Harvesting

Pick the blooms as they open. They are not suitable for drying.

Using

Borage adds a cool, cucumber-like flavour to summer drinks. The flowers and young leaves can be used to garnish salads, dips, and cucumber soups.

Chervil

Chervil is a native of the Middle East, Russia and the Caucasus. However, it has spread to warmer climates where it now grows wild. It was brought to England by the Romans who used it as a medicinal herb, thought to have blood cleansing and other restorative virtues.

Clusters of tiny white flowers populate this hardy annual from spring through to summer, while the foliage is light green and fern like, often turning a pale purple. The foliage gives off a sweet and distinctive smell, making it easy to distinguish from cow-parsley, which looks rather similiar.

Growing

The medium sized seeds are rather quick to germinate, especially if they are fresh. I prefer to sow in modular pots of 12 with about a dozen or so seeds to each pot. Cover them with vermiculite, water them well and cover with plastic until the plants are tough. Transfer each whole pot into a 5″ pot to grow on. Chervil does not take kindly to being moved so try to keep this to a minimum. A late sowing will provide leaves throughout the winter.

If growing outside the soil should be light, but with some water retention. If possible Chervil should be sited in a partially shaded position.

Harvesting

Cut the leaves off when the plant is about 6 weeks old or the shoots are 4″ long. If this is done regularly the plants will produce all year round, although they will need to be under cover during the winter months.

Using

Chervil is one of the traditional herbs found in 'fines herbes' which are indispensible in French cookery. Use the leaves in salads, soups, sauces, vegetables, chicken, white fish and egg dishes, and add them just prior to the final stages of cooking to draw out the full flavour.

Chives

Chives are the only member of the onion family that can be found wild in Europe, North America and Australasia. It is one of the most ancient of all known herbs, but it was not until the 16th Century that chives were first grown in gardens in Europe. Their culinary virtues were brought back from China by Marco Polo, where they had been in use since 3,000 BC.

Growing

Sow about 12 seeds in a 1″ module tray with a slight bottom heat of 65°F (19°C) in the early spring. Transfer the modules into pots for selling or into the open ground once the soil has warmed up. The seeds can also be sown outside when the soil has warmed up.

Every 3 years or so, when the clumps will have grown to quite a size, they should be lifted and split into about 12 bulb lots and then replanted 6″ apart. Dig some well-rotted manure or compost into the bed before replanting.

Harvesting

Chives can be harvested throughout the growing season. Simply cut the upper growth of the leaves and store it in a bag in the fridge. Alternatively, cut and freeze it in ice cube trays for use throughout the winter.

Using

Chives must always be added to a dish towards the end of cooking or the flavour will disappear. They can be freshly cut and snipped into omelettes, salads and soups. They can be blended into soft cheeses, or butter or used with grilled fish or lamb. They can also be used to mix with soured cream for a delicious filling for jacket potatoes.

The leaves, or stems, are mildly antiseptic and can also promote digestion when sprinkled onto food. They are also said to cure and prevent scab on animals, blackspot on rose bushes if grown in near proximity and, if planted next to apple trees, will prevent fungal diseases. Planted around chrysanthemums, carrots and tomatoes they will protect against aphid damage and, if infused and sprayed on cucumber crop, will protect them from downy and powdery mildew.

Coriander

Coriander is possibly one of the first cultivated spices used in cooking, with documentation dating back to 5000 BC referring to its use. It is also cited in Sanskrit writings dating from about 1500 BC. It was the Romans who spread it throughout Europe. It is related to parsley, and both the leaves and the seed are commonly used in spicy dishes such as curries.

Growing

If sowing indoors ,do this in 3" pots at any time of the year. If an outdoor site is selected you can plant between March and April. After germination keep the soil moist and thin the plants out when they are approximately 2" in height, but do be careful as the seedlings do not transplant well. Any plants grown indoors need to be harden off and they can then be moved outdoors once all danger of frost has passed. When planting directly into the ground, thin them out to 6" apart.

Harvesting

Pick the leaves as and when you need them and gather the seeds when they ripen. The leaves can be cut and frozen in ice cube trays, but are not great to dry. The seeds can be stored in an air tight jar until needed.

Using

The leaves and seeds are both widely used as an ingredient and garnish in Asian and most spicy cooking, including curries.

Curry leaf

This leaf truly smells just like a curry. It is a fast-growing, deciduous shrub or small tree with deep roots and scented leaves and is well worth the trouble. It can be grown outside in pots during the hottest part of summer where it likes a sheltered place but it does need heated protection for the rest of the year. The most flavourful leaves are produced when the plants are grown in hot and dry conditions.

Growing

You can buy the seeds from specialist nurseries, but germination can take a long time and they require a constant heat of 20°C. You may have more success if you try to root some stem cuttings from actual plants or twigs that are 'semi-ripe.' Cut the stem cleanly at a node and push the cutting a few centimetres into an equal mix of potting compost and aquarium gravel. Leave 3 or 4 leaves just above the surface of the soil and put the cuttings in a propagator or covered pot. Place the pot in a warm and light place, but out of direct sunlight. Rooting will take about 3 weeks.

Once established the plants need a sunny, well-drained spot. They do carry a warning: they may easily outgrow any space you have for designated them!

As the plants grow, keep trimming them regularly to maintain a supply of young leaves for cooking. Water them regularly and feed during the growing season. The plants will have to be brought in over winter and kept at a temperature of 20°C.

Harvesting

Once established you can pick the leaves as you need them. They dry well, so pick a bunch, tie up the stems and hang them upside down in a dark and warm place until completely dry. When ready, remove the leaves and crumble them into a jar. Store in the fridge.

Using

Add a few crumbled, dried or fresh leaves to your cooking. Try it in a parsnip soup or in a curry.

Dill

Often called dillweed or dillseed, dill is a native of Southern Europe and Western Asia and written records refer to its use by Egyptian doctors over 5000 years ago. It has been used as a protection against witchcraft and also to enhance passion.

It is an annual, producing tiny yellow flowers in flattened umbel custers in the summer and has fine, feathery green leaves.

Growing

Dill seeds do not take to being pricked out and if the plant does get upset it will bolt and will miss out on the leaf producing stage of the summer. The seeds may be started in early spring, under cover and using pots or module trays. The seeds are a fair size so they can be spread out, 6 to a module, or several across the top of a pot and then covered lightly with vermiculite. Germination is 2 to 4 weeks. Plant them out at 9″ apart when there is no more fear of frosts.

Alternatively, the seeds can be sown outdoors in the growing area from early spring with the plants thinned to 9″ apart. Several sowings can be made thoughout the summer to ensure that you have a supply of fresh, young leaves.

Keep dill away from any fennel plants as they do cross-pollinate and their flavours will become mixed. Dill likes a well-drained, poorish soil in full sunlight. Do protect again winds. It may be necessary to provide some support as the plants are prone to being blown over.

When digging up the spent plants in the winter, make sure that all the seed heads are taken off before composting, as the seeds are viable for 3 years.

Harvesting

Once the plant has reached maturity, after about 8 weeks, pick the leaves as and when required. Great care is needed in drying out the leaves, so it is easiest to dry the seeds for storage. Cut off the flower heads just as the seeds begin to ripen and tie them upside down with a paper bag tied over the heads. Store the seeds in a screwtop, air tight container.

Using

Dill is a herb that improves the appetite and the digestion. There are times when the seed is used, due to its more pungent flavour, in soups and grills, as well as with boiled or steamed fish. It is also used in lamb stews and rice dishes, as well as for making white wine dill vinegar.

The leaf is used extensively in many dishes as it often brings out the flavour of the food without overpowering its taste. Simply place a flowering head, before it sets seed, in jars of pickled gherkins and cucumbers to make dill pickles. The leaves can also be boiled with new potatoes and added to egg and salmon dishes. It is the main ingredient of the Scandinavian fish dish, gravadlax.

Dill is used as an antispasmodeic and light sedative. Dill tea is often used for an upset stomach, hiccups and as an appetite stimulant. It can also be used for nursing mothers, to help with the flow of milk and dill water is added to gripe water and other children's medicines because of its capacity to relieve both flatulence and colic.

The seed is also an ideal altnative to salt.

Dill Tea

Steep a teaspoon full of seeds in a cup of boiling water, then strain and drink it.

English Mace

This mace is not the husk of the nutmeg. It is a hardy perennial which produces clusters of small cream flowers. The leaves are brightish green, long and narrow with deep serrations. Although it is called English Mace it was discovered in Switzerland in 1798. It is now grown widely in Northern temperate countries.

Growing

This plant is best propagated by cuttings. Take soft wood

cuttings in late summer, protecting them against wilt as they will be very soft. Plant them out in a bark type compost and cover well with glass or plastic. When the plants are well rooted, harden them off and then either pot up or plant out in the garden, 1 plant per square foot.

You can also propagate by division in the spring or autumn. Re-plant them in a well-prepared bed. It is a hardy plant and shouldn't need any protection, but if you should leave it a bit late in the autumn and frosts are predicted, it is best to winter the divided plants in a cold frame or cold greenhouse.

It prefers a sunny, well-drained site, although I have known others grow it on very heavy soil and produce good crops. It starts off with a cluster of low growing leaves which then produce a series of long stems, culminating in flower heads in the summer. If this flush of flowers is cut down in time, a second supply of leaves and even a second flush of flowers is possible. This plant may be staked in exposed, windy sites. It is usually free from pest and diseases.

Harvesting

Cut fresh leaves whenever they are required. For freezing, cut just before flowering and freeze in small lots. The flowers can be picked throughout the summer. Bunch them in small bundles and hang them upside down to dry. Both the flowers and leaves dry very well. The dry flowers also sell very well for the cut flower market.

Using

The leaves of this herb have a mild but warming, aromatic flavour that mixes well with most other herbs. The chopped leaves can be used in stuffings for chicken, to flavour soups and stews and for sprinkling on potato salads, rice and pasta dishes.

Ginger

Ginger is a low-growing tropical plant, not usually associated with English herbs, but it is one which is used frequently nowadays, and which is easily grown indoors during the summer months in the UK.

You can grow ginger plants from the green ginger you will readily find in supermarkets, but you are not likely to produce a big crop of rhizhomes. Ginger cannot be grown outdoors in the UK as it needs a minimum temperature of 28°C.

Growing

Existing ginger plants can be divided and the roots grown on, although they are difficult to keep alive during the UK winter because of low light levels. Buy some fresh ginger root in the shops but be selective and choose roots which show a shoot bud developing. The shoot bud will look like a small horn at the end of the root. Cut off at least 2″ from this bud.

Take the root and push it into a loam-based compost with the bud upwards. Keep warm and constantly moist during the growing season and move to a larger pot as the plant grows. Ultimately you may need a 15″ pot if it takes well. Once the ginger has started to grow, feed it every two to three weeks with a general pot plant feed.

Harvesting

In the autumn, reduce the watering and let the pots dry out. This will encourage the plants to form rhizhomes. Lift the rhizhomes carefully and use them in cooking.

Using

Cut, peel and slice when needed and put the root back in the fridge where it will keep for a couple of weeks. You can also grate and freeze it so that you always have a plentiful supply. It's a lovely and warming addition to a carrot soup if used in moderation and makes a refreshing tea.

Hyssop

This plant is also known as the Giant Hyssop or Fennel Hyssop.

Growing

The very fine seeds will need heat to germinate (65°F 17°C). Cover them lightly with perlite or vermiculite.

Germination will take about 15 days, but this can be as little as 10 days or as long as 20.

The seeds can be grown outdoors in the early autumn when the soil is still warm, but protection is needed for the young plants. When the seedlings are large enough to handle, prick them out or pot on using a bark based compost. Plants can be planted out in mid-spring when the soil has warmed up.

Harvesting

Cut the flowers for drying just as they begin to open, and cut the leaves just before the late spring flowering. The seeds can be collected when the flower heads turn brown. As soon as the seed is dropping, pick and hang them upside down with a paper bag tied over the heads to catch the seed.

Using

The leaves can be used in salads. They also make a refreshing tea. They can also be added to various summer fruit cups in the same way as borage, or chopped and used in stuffings for pork and in savoury rice. The flowers are useful in fruit salads.

Korean Mint is part of the same family and makes a very refreshing tea. It is reputed to be an excellent 'morning after' tea for an over-indulgent night before.

They are also a useful addition to any pot pourri.

Ladies Mantle

A native of the mountains of Europe, it is happy in either damp or dry shady spots. The crystal dew that lies on the leaves has been reputed to have healing properties. During the medieval period it was dedicated to the Virgin Mary and nickmaned 'a woman's best friend' and was used to regulate a woman's menstrual cycle and to ease the menopause. It is still prescribed by herbalists today.

Growing

This is a hardy perennial. Sow the very fine seeds into prepared seed trays and cover them lightly with vermiculite. No heat is required. Germination can be either sparse or prolific, usually taking up to 3 weeks or more. When sowing in autumn the plants must be over-wintered and planted out when the frosts are over at about 18″ apart.

Harvesting

Pick young leaves after the dew has gone off, for use thoughout the summer months. For drying as a plant, cut just as the plant comes into flower.

Using

Tear the young leaves into small pieces and toss them into salads.

It is used by herbalists for menstrual problems and can be used as a mouthwash after teeth have been pulled. The leaves can also be boiled for a green wool dye or used in veterinary medicine for the treatment of diarrhoea.

Lemon Verbena

First introduced into Europe during the 1800s by the Spanish who discovered it in Chile, lemon verbena was prized for its wonderful perfume. It is a half-hardy, deciduous perennial with tiny white flowers tinged with lilac in the early summer, with pale green, spear shaped leaves, strongly scented with lemon.

Growing

The seeds of lemon vebena are usually sown in sets. Sow in the spring in module trays and cover lightly with vermiculite. Place them in a propagator with a bottom heat of 60°F (15°C). When the seedlings are large enough to handle, prick them out into 3½″ pots using a bark/grit mix of compost. Do not plant them out from these pots for at least 2 years.

These plants do not like frosts, cold winds or temperatures below 60°F (15°C), so they will need protection from all of these. This can be done by a thick mulch around the root area. In the spring, give the plants a gentle pruning and revive them by spraying with warm water. Once the plant has started re-shooting, remove the dead tips and prune them gently to encourage new growth.

Harvesting

Pick the leaves at any time. The leaves will dry very quickly and easily, whilst keeping both their colour and scent. Store the dried leaves in an air tight screw-top jar.

Using

Fresh leaves can be used to flavour oils, vinegars, drinks, fruit puddings, apple jelly, cakes, stuffings and confectionery. Used as a refreshing tea it will soothe bronchial congestion. It definitely has some slight sedative properties, but avoid long term usage as it is possible for stomach erosion to occur.

Marjoram/Oregano

The 3 most common varieties are 'wild marjoram' (common oregano), pot marjoram and sweet, or knotted, marjoram. Associated mostly with Italian food, particularly pizzas, it is highly likely that the plant actually originated from Greece. The name in Greek means 'joy of the mountain.'

Growing

Marjoram grows well indoors in 3″ pots or sown directly in the ground in partial shade or sun in March/April. Sow the seeds 1″ apart and press them into the soil surface. They are so tiny that it is difficult to sow the seeds individually. You will therefore have to transplant clumps of seedlings every 6 to 8″ inches in the open. Thin these to 3 clumps of 3 to 4 plants per pot if growing in containers. Harden off the plants raised indoors and then move them outdoors once all danger of frost has passed. Finally, when the plants have reached 2″ tall, thin them out to one clump 12″ apart.

Harvesting

The leaves can be harvested at any time. Cut the leafy stems at flowering for drying. Wild marjoram is best used as a dried herb. Pick the leaves on a dry day and place them in a dark, dry and warm place until they have dried. Then store them in an air tight container either as whole or crumbled leaves. They will retain their flavour for three months or more. Sweet marjoram, however, is best used fresh, so just pick it as required.

Using

Marjoram can be used as a substitute for oregano in most dishes. It is also good sprinkled onto pizzas and vegetable dishes.

Marsh Mallow

Also known as sweet weed, marsh malice, and wymote, marsh mallow is found scattered all over the world, usually on salt marshes and on banks and dunes near the sea. It has been known for hundreds of years with the Romans using it as a tasty vegetable as well as a stuffing for baby pigs. In later years herbalists were said to have used marsh mallow to cure toothache, sore throats and abdominal pains.

It is a hardy perennial with pinkish white flowers that appear in the late summer/early autumn. The grey/green leaves are tear shaped and covered with fine hairs.

Growing

The seeds are sown during the autumn into prepared module trays. Cover them with a light sprinkle of vermiculite and winter them outside, under glass. Germination takes place in spring and is inclined to be erratic. Plant them out 18″ apart once the plants are big enough to handle. Divide mature plants for replanting into fresh, prepared beds in either spring or autumn.

Harvesting

As the leaves do not keep well, pick them fresh and as required. Dig up the roots of 2 year old plants in the autumn, after the tops have died down. These roots can then be used either fresh or dried.

Using

Use the flowers and leaves in salads. The leaves can be added to oil and vinegar to give it extra flavour. Alternatively, the fresh leaves can be steamed and used as a vegetable. The roots may be boiled until soft and then peeled and fried in butter.

An infusion of the leaves or flowers makes a soothing gargle, while an infusion of the roots can be used for the treatment of coughs, diarrhoea or insomnia. Marsh-Mallow is also said to to cure inflamation and ulceration of the stomach and the small intestine and sore throats as well as removing the pain from cystitis.

Mint

Mint is an ancient and well regarded herb. It was sought after for its refreshing fragrance as much as for its legendary powers as an aid to seduction. Mint was grown in early English gardens, and was probably brought to Britain in Roman Times. Apicius, in his famous cook book written in the 1st Century, lists mint in many dishes. Charlemagne (742-814) decreed in 812 that many acres of mint, together with other herbs, be grown in his famous gardens of seventy-eight herbs.

There are many varieties of mint: spearmint (*mentha spicata*) - a traditional mint for mint sauces, ginger mint, pinapple mint, chocolate mint and apple mint. Some smell wonderful but can be dissappointing once picked.

Growing

Sow indoors anytime from February to June. It can be sown

outdoors but germination may be slow. Seeds should be sown very thinly by pressing the seeds into moist compost, then place in sealed polythene bags or covered with glass. Water them from beneath and keep the compost moist, but not very wet.

After germination, remove the bag or from under the glass and grow on. If your plants are pot grown, transplant them to 1 plant per 3″ pot. Harden them off and finally move them outdoors once all danger of frost has passed.

Because of mint's invasive habit, the creeping roots can be easily propagated, either directly into the ground or in pots. However, because mint is such a strong-growing plant, it can easily kill other nearby plants. You are therefore best planting it in a container or sinking a bottomless flowerpot into the ground.

Harvesting

Mint can be harvested continuously throughout the growing season. Cut the top leaves first because this will encourage the plant to shoot out again further down the stem. Never strip the plant of all it's leaves.

It is possible to store the leaves in a warm place to dry, but some of the flavour will certainly disappear.

Mint Sauce
Pick some fresh mint leaves. Mix them with a small amount of vinegar and sugar and, with the back of a teaspoon,

bruise the mint to bring out the flavour.

Mint Jelly

Peel and cut 5lb of cooking apples into thick chunks (unpeeled/un-cored) and put them into a large saucepan together with 40fl oz of water and 8 tablespoons of freshly chopped mint. Bring to the boil, then simmer gently for 45 minutes until the fruit is soft, stirring from time to time.

Add 40fl oz of distilled malt vinegar to the pan and boil for a further 5 minutes. Then spoon the apple mixture into a jelly bag or a cheesecloth and leave it to strain into a large bowl for at least 12 hours. I tie the cheesecloth up with string and hang it from the handles of the overhead cupboards in the kitchen overnight, dripping into a bowl. It may look strange, but it certainly does the trick.

Discard the pulp remaining in the jelly bag. Measure the liquid in the bowl and return it to a saucepan, together with 1lb of sugar for each 20fl oz. of liquid. Heat this gently, stirring until the sugar has dissolved, then raise the heat to boil rapidly. After about 10 minutes, remove from the heat and test for a set.

Skim the surface with a slotted spoon, then stir in the chopped mint. Allow it to cool slightly, then stir it well to distribute the mint. Ladle it into warm jars, cover and seal them and label appropriately. The jars can be sterilised by placing them in boiling water, then drying them off in the oven.

Mustard

Mustard is regarded as the 'king of condiments' and has been used to spice up food for many thousands of years. It has also always been a popular 'first to grow' for children, because it is both easy and fast growing. The leaves are great raw, either in salads or as a cooked greens. They are nutritious and healthy. It is the seeds which are harvested to make the condiment that you use on hotdogs, sandwiches, and which are ground and used in curries together with coriandar seeds.

Growing

Mustard plants grow well in most good soils and prefer a full sun but cool weather. If you plant them weekly, you will have a continuous crop. Sow the seeds in the spring ¼" deep and 3" apart. Thin the seedlings to 5 - 9" apart and separate the rows to 1ft apart. Do not plant in the height of summer.

Use plenty of water and fertilizer/compost to promote the fast growth of tender, green leaves. Keep the plants well weeded so that weeds do not compete for water and nutrients. It also makes harvesting easier, too.

Harvesting

Mustard greens are best eaten raw. Pick the leaves when they are young and tender. The leaves can become tough and may have a strong flavour during hot, dry weather.

When the plants begin to yellow, you can collect the mustard seeds. Leave them on the plants as long as possible, but do harvest before the pods burst open and spill the seeds. In my opinion these are the best bits of the plant and they can really pep up a curry.

Using

Pick the leaves as and when required to add to salads.

Ground Mustard
Use dried mustard seeds for this. Place them in a coffee grinder or a food processor. Grind them until they are of a very fine, powdery consistency. Store the powder in a bag or a small jar, along with your other spices.

Mustard Condiment
Use dried mustard seeds of which there are a variety. White, or yellow seeds can both make a yellow mustard. Brown seeds make a stronger, more pungent brown mustard.

Place the seeds and a small amount of water or vinegar into a blender. Avoid using too much liquid, or it will be runny. You can also use almost any liquid, including wine or even beer. Run the blender until the mixture is smooth and store the mustard in the refrigerator.

Parsley

Parsley is very possibly the most popular herb grown in this country. It is, however, also one of the harder herbs to grow. This is partly because it is neither quick nor easy to germinate as many other herbs. It also requires a reasonably rich soil to perform well. The saying goes that parsley visits the devil 7 times before it germinates. Traditionally it has been documented as a curative and was known by Beatrix Potter's Peter Rabbit, of whom it was said, *"First he ate some lettuce and some broad beans, then some radishes, and then, feeling rather sick, he went to look for some parsley."*

Growing

If sowing indoors, plant in small 3″ pots any time between February and April. Outdoors, plant in open ground in a rich soil and approximately 2 weeks before the last frost. It is a notoriously slow germinator and can take anything up to 40 days, so be patient and remember that it must visit the devil 7 times!

Sow the seeds 1″ apart and ¼″ deep and, after germination, keep the compost moist but not wet. When the plants reach 1″ they can be transplanted to 1 plant per 3″ pot. Harden off plants which have been raised indoors and then move them outdoors, once all danger of frost has passed.

Harvesting

Cut the parsley when the leaves are of a suitable size. Leaves can be used either fresh or dried and you can keep harvesting them throughout the season. Do keep on top of it or it will run to seed. Be aware that parsley seeds can also be used in some recipes.

Using

Parsley is extremely versatile and can be used in almost all recipes. It goes with almost everything, including omelets, salads, stews, vegetables, fish, sauces, eggs and soups and is therefore an ideal herb to use as a garnish. It is one of the basic herbs used in a bouquet garni.

You can freeze parsley for use during the winter by chopping up the leaves, placing them in an ice-cube tray, topping up with water and freezing. Take the cubes out on when needed. This can be done with most herbs and also with crushed garlic and ginger.

Pepper | Black

Apart from salt, pepper is the most commonly used seasoning in the kitchen. It is a tropical vine which can be grown indoors in the UK. With patience and good cultivation you can grow this as a houseplant to produce your own peppercorns. Pepper will not survive outdoors, even during the summer. It is grown more for novelty value in this country than for any functional use.

Sowing

Sow the seeds from an established plant. The plant will need several years of growth before it will be mature enough to bear 'fruit.'

Rosemary

Rosemary is a decorative, as well as functional, herb and it is well worth growing for its appearance alone. Dependant on the variety, it has small, profuse flowers which appear in late spring and which range from a dark blue through pale blue and right down to white.

Growing

Rosemary will thrive on a sandy, light soil and requires relatively little maintainence. It can tolerate most soil conditions as long as they are not water-logged, but it does prefer sunny, sheltered conditions. It will stand severe frosts if conditions are not also windy and wet as well.

Sow it thinly indoors in 3″ pots during February to April, or directly into open ground after the last frost, 1″ apart and ¼″ deep. It can take up to 30 days to germinate. After germination, keep the compost moist but not wet.
Thin out the plants after they have reached 1" and transfer them to a larger pot. Harden off any plants which have

been raised indoors and finally move them outdoors once all danger of frost has passed. Thin them out to 18″ apart but one plant should be more than sufficient for most household needs, except when used as decorative hedging or to sell.

Harvesting

Harvest the leaves as required. You can also use the mature stems and the strips of the leaves as skewers for meat kebabs. The leaves can be used either fresh or dried.

Using

Rosemary can be used fresh or dried in cooking. It is always best used straight from the garden, but it can be kept in the fridge for up to a week or so.

It is often associated with lamb, but it goes equally well with pork and poultry. It is used in stuffings as well as simply letting the whole sprig infuse with the natural juices at the bottom of the roasting pan, and it goes exceptionally well with roast potatoes. But then, what doesn't!

Rosemary can also be used to flavour salad dressings. You can add a sprig to a bottle of white wine vinegar. Leave it in a dark cupboard for a week to let the flavour infuse. Add it to oil to make a salad dressing.

Sage

Sage sown from seed is slow to establish. Common sage is, however, hardy and tolerant of almost all conditions as long as it receives a regular dose of full sun.

It was thought to impart wisdom and improve one's memory and the English herbalist and author of *'The Herball, or Generall Historie of Plantes (1597)'* wrote that, *"Sage is singularly good for the head and brain, it quickeneth the senses and memory, strengtheneth the sinews, restoreth health to those that have the palsy, and taketh away shakey trembling of the members.* Folklore also says that the wife rules the household when sage grows well in the garden.

Growing

If growing indoors, plant thinly in 3″ pots or trays between February and April. Sow the seeds 1″ apart and ¼″ deep. After germination keep the compost moist but not wet.

When the plants are 1″ tall, thin them out to 1 plant per 3″ pot. Harden off plants which have been raised indoors and finally move them outdoors once all danger of frost has passed. Re-pot them into larger pots in stages up to 12″ or so and, if planting in the ground, thin them out to 8″ apart.

Harvesting

Harvest the leaves either before or at flowering time, as and when when you need them. They can be dried by trying them in bunches and hanging them upside down in a warm, dry and dark place.

Using

Sage is very popular in stuffings for both poultry and pork and can be adapted to many different stuffing recipes using breadcrumbs, dried fruits, and sausagemeat.

Thyme

Thyme comes in many varieties and should be planted in every garden both for its delicious scent and its versatility in the kitchen. The Greeks gave thyme several beneficial attributes, including using it to restore strength and clarity to the mind, and also its ability to clear the air of illness and disease.

There are a few varieties of thyme, all with a unique scent. Golden-scented thyme (*thymus pulegioides*) is a slightly lemon scented thyme, great for cooking and with lavender coloured flowers. Garden thyme (*thymus vulgaris*) was the original thyme used for flavouring and has been grown for hundreds of years. Thyme (*thymus serpyllum*) or ground cover thyme is great for cooking and is also great for ground cover.

Growing

Sow thinly in 3″ pots any time between March and April, keeping the pots indoors. Cover them with a thin layer of compost, water them well and place in a sealed polythene bag or cover with glass. Water them from beneath.

Remove them from the bags or glass after germination and place them in a light position, but out of direct sunlight. Thin them to 3 plants per pot when the plants are about ½″ tall.

Harden them off and finally move them outdoors once all danger of frost has passed. Once the plants are established with a good root system, divide them into separate plants and pot each one up into 6″ pots or directly into the ground in full sun.

Harvesting

Harvest whole stems either before or at flowering time. Thyme is easy to dry and keep.

Using

Thyme is one of the most fragrant herbs and goes well with fish, meat, poultry, game and cheese. It is also used in bouquet garni.

Yarrow

Also known as nosebleed and with several other local names, this hardy perennial carries small white flowers slightly tinged with pink during the summer and autumn. Its name, *millefolium*, means 1000 leaves which is a very good description of the dark green, aromatic, feather-like leaves. This is an ancient herb that was used by the Greeks to control haemorrages and it is still widely used today in herbal medicine.

Growing

For best results, plant the small seed under cool protection in autumn. Leave the trays in a cool greenhouse for the winter. The germination can, however, be very erratic. Harden the plants off and plant them out in the spring. In either spring or early autumn mature plants can be dug up and seperated into smaller plants and replanted. This will also curb the invasive nature of the plant.

Yarrow is often used as a companion plant as its root secretions can activate resistance to disease in others close by. It is often said that herbs grown near yarrow often deepen their flavour and aroma, as well as building up their medicinal properties.

You can infuse yarrow in boiling water to make a copper fertiliser.

Harvesting

Cut the leaves and flowers for drying just as they come into flower.

Using

The young leaves can be used in salads. But yarrow's greatest single asset is its well known and documented medicinal properties. As a hot infusion it will produce sweats that can cool down fevers and expel toxins. It can also be made up into a decoction for open wounds, chapped skin and rashes.

A warning!
Yarrow should always be taken in moderation and never for long periods as it can produce itching of the skin. Large doses can produce both vertigo and headaches. Pregnant women should not take yarrow.

Watercress

You will either love it or hate it. Watercress has a hot, pepper-like taste and is related to the nasturtium family. It grows in semi-aquatic conditions along the edges of streams. The plants grow partially submerged under water. They produce small white flowers all summer long and prefer cool weather, but out in the full sun.

Growing

Grow watercress from seed. Plant it indoors in a rich seed starting soil and keep the soil moist. Once big enough to transplant, move it to the side of a slow flowing waterbed.

Harvesting

Once the plant has flowered the leaves and stems become too bitter to eat, so cut it before blooming. They will keep in the fridge for several days.

Using

Watercress is used in salads and as a garnish and also makes a lovely soup. It has been used for both bladder and kidney problems.

Wild Garlic

Wild Garlic is often referred to as wood garlic, onion flower and bear's garlic. It is native to both Europe and Asia and is naturalized in many countries. A hardy perennial, it has clusters of white flowers during spring and summer and, along with nettles, is the introduction to 'free food' for many novice foragers.

Growing

It is best sown directly into the site where you want the plants to grow. Split the established plant in the autumn, after the flowers have died back, and if the plants are becoming invasive in spring, simply remove them.

Using

Pick from the end of spring for use in salads, soups and as a vegetable. It is also used as a traditional household disinfectant. The roots may be boiled until soft and then peeled and fried in butter and an infusion of the leaves or flowers makes a soothing gargle, while an infusion of the roots can be used for the treatment of coughs, diarrhoea or insomnia.

Appendix

Companion Planting

Companion planting is the method adopted where different plants are deliberately planted together so that the presence of one will dramatically improve the growth of other. This can be because one may repel or attract pests, offer shade or add nutrients to the soil.

Some plants will even produce scents in order to protect themselves from pests. It makes sense, therefore, to place these plants next to another plant that is vulnerable to the same pests, but which doesn't produce this same natural deterrent. The carrot root fly, for example, does not like the scent of onions, but loves carrots. The strong smell emitted by the onions hides the scent of the carrots.

You can strategically plant a 'honey pot' next to your prize crop. For instance, slugs love lettuce. They also love marigolds, so use the marigolds as a sacrifice by planting them around the bed of lettuces.

In fact, marigolds are very good to have around your vegetable plot. They attract hoverflies and hoverfly larvae like aphids. (A hoverfly larvae will eat as many as 800 aphids before it pupates). Ladybirds are also very good at eating aphids, so attract them with plants like dill and fennel.

Below is a list of common vegetables and their ideal companion plants, or herbs.

Crop	Companion
Asparagus	Tomatoes, parsley and basil
Beans	Most vegetables and herbs
Broad beans	Potatoes, cucumbers, and celery
Runner beans	Radish
Cabbage family	Herbs, celery and beetroot
Carrots	Peas, lettuce and onions
Celery	Onions and tomatoes
Cucumbers	Beans, corn, peas and radish
Aubergines	Broad beans and marigolds
Lettuce	Carrots, radish and cucumbers
Corn	Potatoes, broad beans and peas
Melons	Corn, nasturtiums and radish
Onion family	Beetroot, carrots and lettuce
Parsley	Tomatoes and asparagus
Peas	Carrots, radish and cucumbers
Potatoes	Beans, horseradish and corn
Pumpkins	Corn and marigolds
Radish	Peas, lettuce and cucumber
Spinach	Cauliflower and celery
Squashes	Nasturtiums, corn and marigolds
Strawberries	Broad Beans, lettuce, onions and spinach
Tomatoes	Basil, onions and nasturtiums
Turnips	Peas

This chart identifies common herbs, the plants they are paired with and what they repel. It is by no means an exhaustive list, but it does show the main ones.

Herb	Partnered with	Repels
Allium	Veg and fruit trees	aphids, carrot flies & moles
Basil	Tomatoes	Flies
Borage	Tomatoes	Tomato worm
Catnip	Aubergine	Ants
Coriander	All veg	Aphids
Chives	Carrots	Root flies
Feverfew	Roses	aphids
Garlic	Roses	aphids
Marigolds	Most veg	aphids
Mint	Cabbage and tomatoes	cabbage white butterflies, aphids & flea beetles
Mustard	Cabbage, cauliflower, radish, sprouts, turnips and kohl rabi	Attracts many pests
Nasturtiums	Radishes, Cabbage, squashes, pumpkins and fruit trees	Aphids, squash bugs and striped pumpkin beetles
Oregano	Brassicas	Cabbage butterflies
Rosemary	Cabbage, beans, carrots and sage	Cabbage butterflies, bean beetles and carrot flies
Sage	Rosemary, cabbage, and carrots	Cabbage moths, carrot flies, flea beetles and slugs
Thyme	Cabbage	Cabbage worms
Yarrow	Plant near aromatic herbs to enhance the production of essential oils.	Attracts hover flies and their larvae which prey on aphids

Storing your Produce

This isn't a treatise on storing produce; that would be a completely new book in itself. It is more a case of a few jottings from someone who has been caught out on more than one occasion, and it's all very well planting, harvesting, preparing and cooking, but as so much of your produce will be ready at the same time, it makes it impossible to use everything.

There is always room for exchanging or bartering on the allotment, but even so, I advise and implore you to give thought and consideration to how you will preserve your excess produce, even before you go out to buy the seeds. If you don't, you will certainly have a glut and, believe me, it's very easy to get fed up with parsnip soup.

First, consider your own freezer capacity, your cupboards, to store the empty bottles and jars you've been collecting as well as where they might go when full and dry, warm places for hanging herbs etc.

On top of this, you must take your own energy levels and time into account. No matter how enjoyable making chutneys and soups is, harvesting and preparing your vegetables will indeed take time and it can be very tiring, so plan ahead!

A Small Note on Composting

There is so much information and talk about composting that you would think that some kind of wonderful alchemy takes place inside that black plastic bin or compost heap. Mind you, in a way it does!

Composting is simply an effective and resourceful way of recycling your organic produce back into the soil. There is little point in throwing it out for the weekly (or now fortnightly) waste removal. You might as well make use of it to help you to grow your next year's vegetables.

There is, however, no magic formula or recipe; much of it is just common sense. Too much veg will create slime, as anyone who has left vegetables in the bottom of the fridge knows. You therefore have to add some 'fibre' and the cardboard from your toilet rolls, egg boxes (the compressed cardboard ones) and even used kitchen towel are all ideal; as long as it hasn't got meat either in it or on it.

You can use chemicals to induce quick composting, but personally I always feel that that it defeats the object. It is much more satisfying to be able to spade out from the bottom, the very finest, richest, earthiest and crumbliest compost of all time, in the knowledge that you made it and it was free.

Composting with Worms

Composting with worms is an efficient and environmentally friendly way to get rid of waste and give the nutrients back to your soil. What's more, worm composting is easier than just relying on a compost heap as a wormery; once built and filled it doesn't need as much attention. You can also keep a wormery indoors - something you really wouldn't want to do with a compost heap!

Basically the worms eat the scraps which become compost as they pass through the worm's body. The compost is exited from the worm at the tail end. The 'compost' is actually called vermicompost.

In a nutshell a wormery comprises of a special bin, bedding - freshly made vermicompost is ideal but you can also use shredded newspaper, straw, leaf mould, corrugated cardboard - and worms, of course. The more the merrier, as more worms equals faster processing of your waste.

The wormery can process most of your kitchen waste, although there is a cautionary tale with regard to dairy products, which should be avoided, not because the worms cannot process them, but because of the unwanted vermin and flies that may be attracted to the wormery.

Resources

It is well worth scrutinising the seed catalogues every year. You will find out what's new and what's successful. All the big companies insert their catalogues in the gardening magazines and newspapers. These are great resources and are also easily accessible. I've listed here a few of the smaller companies who give a fantastic, personalised service, as I'm all in favour of supporting the small, family run business.

The Real Seed Company
Brithdir Mawr Farm, Newport, Nr. Fishguard,
Pembrokeshire, SA42 0QJ
Tel. 01239 821107 | www.realseeds.co.uk
A friendly family run company that grows the seeds they sell, so they know all about them.

The Organic Gardening Catalogue
Riverdene Business Park, Molesey Road, Hersham,
Surrey, KT12 4RG
Tel. 0845 1301304 | www.organiccatalog.com
A well respected company specialising in organic seeds. They also provide compost made from recycled peat.

Suffolk Herbs
Monks Farm, Kelvedon, Colchester, Essex, CO5 9PG
Tel. 01376 572456 | www.suffolkherbs.co.uk
An independent company who offer one of the largest selections of organic and natural herb seeds in Europe.

Seeds by Size
45, Couchfield, Hemel Hempstead, Herts., HP1 1PA
Tel. 01442 251458 | www.seeds-by-size.co.uk
A great company selling a wide range of seeds and by weight, not by packet, so you can have as many, or as little, as you like.

Tamar Organics
Cartha Martha Farm, Rezare, Launceston, PL15 9NX
Tel. 01579 371087 | www.tamarorganics.co.uk
Approved by the Soil Association, Tamar Organics has an easy to use website (at least so I'm told - I wouldn't know!) All their plant material, artichokes, onions, garlic and potatoes are 100% organic and none of the seeds they offer are either GM or treated.

Victoriana Nursery Gardens
Challock, Nr. Ashford, Kent, TN25 4DG
Tel. 01233 740529 | www.victoriananursery.co.uk
A true working production nursery and plant centre with nearly 50 years of experience.

Polytunnels and Greenhouses

First Tunnels
Dixon Street, Barrowford, Lancashire, BB9 8PL
Tel. 01282 601253 | www.firsttunnels.co.uk

Five Star Polytunnels
Unit 2 Cellan, Lampeter, Ceredigion, SA48 8HU
Tel. 01570 421580 | www.polytunnels.me.uk

Haxnicks
Haxnicks Ltd., Beaumont Business Centre, Woodlands
Road, Mere, Wiltshire, BA12 6BT
Tel. 0845 241 1555 | www.haxnicks.co.uk

Chaselink
New Street, Burntwood, Staffs., WS7 8BS
Tel. 01543 459655 | www.chaselink.co.uk

General Supplies

Ascott Smallholding Supplies
Units 9/10, The Old Creamery, Four Crosses,
Llanymynech, SY22 6LP
Tel. 0845 130 6285 | www.ascott.biz
An Aladdin's cave of all sorts of equipment for the
smallholder and horticulturist.

Wiggly Wigglers
Lower Blakemere Farm, Blakemere, Herefordshire
HR2 9PX
Tel. 01981 500391 | wiggly@wigglywigglers.co.uk
A great first introduction to worms and composting.

Metric/Imperial Conversion Chart

It's always best to remember a formula for converting imperial to metric and, hopefully, this guide will help you to convert the various gardening and cooking instructions in both this, and possibly many other books.

When you know	Multiply by	To Find
Millimetres	25	Inches
Centimetres	2.5	Inches
Centimetres	30	Feet
Metres	0.9	Yards
Inches	0.393	Centimetres
Yards	1.1	Metres
Miles	0.6	Kilometres
Grams	28	Ounces
Kilograms	0.45	Pounds
Ounces	0.035	Grams
Pounds	2.2	Kilograms
Millilitres	30	Fluid Ounces
Litres	0.568	Pints
Litres	4.546	Gallons

The Good Life Press Ltd., PO Box 536, Preston,
PR2 9ZY   Tel. 01772 652693
www.thegoodlifepress.co.uk

The Good Life Press Ltd. publishes books for the
farmer, smallholder and country dweller.
Other titles of interest:

The Pocket Guide to Wild Food
Flowerpot Farming
The Polytunnel Companion
The Cheese Making Book
The Sausage Book
The Smoking and Curing Book
How to Butcher Livestock and Game
A Guide to Traditonal Pig Keeping
The Bread and Butter Book
First Buy a Field
Making Jams and Preserves
Precycle!
and many more

We also publish the monthly magazine, Home Farmer,
aimed at anyone who wants a slice of the good life,
whether they live in the city or the country.
www.homefarmer.co.uk

HomeFarmer for dreamers and realists